The Comedy Improv Handbook

The Comedy Improv Handbook: A Comprehensive Guide to University Improvisational Comedy in Theatre and Performance is a one-stop resource for both improv teachers and students, covering improv history, theory, maxims, exercises, games, and structures. You will learn the necessary skills and techniques needed to become a successful improviser, developing a basic understanding of the history of improvisation and its major influences, structures, and theories. This book also addresses issues associated with being a college improviser – like auditions, rehearsals, performances, and the dynamics of improv groups.

- Features a skills list and teaching tips for each game and performance structure, clarifying the core needs of each.
- Contains exercises to help you build the skills necessary for effective two-person improv scenes.
- Covers the craft of long form improv, from editing and callbacks to group scenes.

Matt Fotis is an Assistant Professor of Theatre at Albright College where he teaches improvisation, acting, and writing for performance. He is the author of Long Form Improvisation & American Comedy – The Harold. His work has appeared in Theatre Journal, Theatre Topics, The Journal of American Drama & Theatre, The Encyclopedia of Humor Studies, The Encyclopedia of American Studies, and MLB.com, among others. He is also an award-winning playwright.

Siobhan O'Hara is a graduate from Albright College and former president of Albright Improv. She is continuing her education and training at The Upright Citizens Brigade.

Bound to Create

You are a creator.

Whatever your form of expression — photography, filmmaking, animation, games, audio, media communication, web design, or theatre — you simply want to create without limitation. Bound by nothing except your own creativity and determination.

Focal Press can help.

For over 75 years Focal has published books that support your creative goals. Our founder, Andor Kraszna-Krausz, established Focal in 1938 so you could have access to leading-edge expert knowledge, techniques, and tools that allow you to create without constraint. We strive to create exceptional, engaging, and practical content that helps you master your passion.

Focal Press and you.

Bound to create.

We'd love to hear how we've helped you create. Share your experience:
www.focalpress.com/boundtocreate

Focal Press
Taylor & Francis Group

The Comedy Improv Handbook

A Comprehensive Guide to University Improvisational Comedy in Theatre and Performance

Matt Fotis
Siobhan O'Hara

Focal Press
Taylor & Francis Group

NEW YORK AND LONDON

First published 2016
by Focal Press
711 Third Avenue, New York, NY 10017

and by Focal Press
2 Park Square, Milton Park, Abingdon, Oxon OX14 4RN

Focal Press is an imprint of the Taylor & Francis Group, an informa business

© 2016 Taylor & Francis

The right of Matt Fotis and Siobhan O'Hara to be identified as authors of this work has been asserted by them in accordance with sections 77 and 78 of the Copyright, Designs and Patents Act 1988.

Library of Congress Cataloging in Publication Data
Fotis, Matt, 1979-
The comedy improv handbook : a comprehensive guide to university improvisational comedy in theatre and performance / Matt Fotis, Siobhan O'Hara.
pages cm
Includes index.
1. Improvisation (Acting)—Vocational guidance. 2. Improvisation (Acting)—Study and teaching (Higher) 3. Comedy—Technique. 4. Stand-up comedy—Vocational guidance. I. O'Hara, Siobhan. II. Title.
PN2071.15F47 2015
792.02'8—dc23
2015021157

ISBN: 978-1-138-93425-2 (hbk)
ISBN: 978-1-138-93423-8 (pbk)
ISBN: 978-1-315-67810-8 (ebk)

Typeset in Giovanni
by Swales & Willis Ltd, Exeter, Devon, UK

Printed and bound by CPI Group (UK) Ltd, Croydon, CR0 4YY

To the teachers and students who have given me so much.

– Matt Fotis

To my loving and supportive parents, Ben and Kathleen O'Hara. Thank you for unintentionally teaching me the basics of improv: Be kind, listen, and share.

– Siobhan O'Hara

Contents

Acknowledgments

As with any project, there were many folks who helped in the creation of this book. We're indebted to the many improv teachers out there past and present, from the legends to the folks teaching improv at the local community center.

Big thanks to Taylor Rae Cole for her section headings and cover design that you'll probably spend more time looking at than anything else.

We would also like to thank the ACRE program at Albright College for providing financial and administrative support for the project (and for helping us to understand what a ligand is and why it is important). Special thanks as well to the Theatre Department and Dr. Julia Matthews, Jeff Lentz, Wayne Vettleson, Paula Trimpey, and David Tanner for championing and supporting improv at Albright.

We would also like to extend a hearty handshake to Logan Toomey for his pun support throughout the project. Last but not least, we must thank Dante for keeping our spirits up through his never-ending motivational words. May you forever be at an outdoor Earth Day concert. YEAH!

Introduction

If you are reading this handbook, chances are you're now a member of a college improv team or taking an improv course. Or you want to be. Or you're still in high school. Or you wish you could go back to college, because really, when else is two classes a day considered full time? Or maybe you're an acting teacher looking to teach (or have been assigned to teach) an improv class. Or an improv teacher looking for a book that doesn't subscribe to one particular theory or process. Or maybe you just want to get back to basics. Or you are a business major looking to become more creative. Or an aspiring teacher looking for new ways to work with your students. Or a scientist looking to improve your communication skills so you can tell the world all of the wonderful things you are doing (and have them actually understand). Whatever your relationship to college improv – Congratulations! You've just discovered an art form that is going to change your life. Call your mother. She misses you. Your father is more than likely disappointed. Or on his way to Buffalo Wild Wings … to drown his disillusionment with you in wings.

So What is This Handbook and Why Should I Read it?

This handbook is a compilation of improv history, theory, maxims, exercises, games, and structures. By reading through this handbook you will learn the necessary skills and techniques to become a successful improviser. You will develop a basic understanding of the history of improvisation, and its major influences, structures, and theories. For those of you in a leadership position (or aspiring toward one), this handbook is also designed to be a teaching tool with categorized exercises and games, along with helpful teaching tips. It also addresses some issues associated with being a college improviser – like auditions, rehearsals, performances, and dating. We've also included a guide to professional training. Let us be clear: reading this handbook alone **won't** make you a better improviser. You need to get on stage and improvise. But reading this handbook **will** give you an array of tools to use from a variety of improv "schools" when you are up on stage.

Wait a Second, Why Should I Listen to You Two?

Good question. So let us tell you a little more about ourselves.

I'm Matt Fotis. I have a PhD. I wrote another book about improv called *Long Form Improvisation and American Comedy: The Harold* (you should really read it. I'd prefer if you bought it and then got ten copies for all of your friends, but if you check it out from the library that's cool too). I've been hooked on improv since I was in college back in the 90s. I've been involved in improv as a performer, coach, teacher,

2

founder, artistic director, workshop coordinator, festival teacher, festival organizer, and judge. As a teacher I've worked with groups at small liberal arts colleges, medium-sized state schools, and large state universities. The groups that I've worked with have all been pretty darn successful. Perhaps I've just been in the right places at the right times, but I think part of the success is due to my teaching.

I'm Siobhan O'Hara. I'm a college improviser. Well, technically I just graduated so now I'm not. But I was. For four years. For two years I served as president of Albright Improv at Albright College. I've done both short form and long form at the college level. So I've been in the thick of college improv. I don't have a PhD, but I've been in your shoes.

Together we bring a nice blend of expertise and real-world experience. So, feel free to listen to what you like, use what works, and make up your own rules. We've also offered up some suggestions for further reading throughout the book to round out your improv library. You know, like Viola Spolin's *Improvisation for the Theatre*. If you haven't read that, put this down, and go read it. Then come back. We'll wait.

Pretty good, right?

Now go watch TJ & Dave live, or in *Trust Us, This is All Made Up*.

They're pretty good, right? Now go read their book with Pam Victor, *Improvisation at the Speed of Life*.

Anything Else I Should Know?

You can take the skills you learn in improv (and in the pages that follow) to the stage, but also to your other worldly ventures. Improv is bigger than just being spontaneously funny: if you are open to it, improv will change your life. Plus, improvisers tend to be intellectually curious, giving, generous, and fun people. So enjoy, and remember:

Have fun.

Take risks.

And be nice to one another.

What is Improv?

You are going to have to answer this question at holidays and on summer break a lot. So let's arm you with an answer. Contrary to your "super-funny" Aunt Shirley's definition, improv is not ad-libbing, winging it, or flying by the seat of your pants. It isn't something you do when you are caught unaware or when you fail to plan. *Not preparing does not equal improvising.* Improv is a style of spontaneous performance. The most prevalent form of improv performed today is what Amy Seham has classified as Chicago-style improv-comedy, which is "a form of unscripted performance that uses audience suggestions to initiate or shape scenes or plays created spontaneously and cooperatively according to agreed-upon rules or game structures, in the presence of an audience—frequently resulting in comedy."[1] Or as Mick Napier more simply states, "improvisation is getting on stage and making stuff up as you go along."[2]

Improv is more than simply a form of performance – *improvisation is a system of creativity, a mindset that focuses on cooperation and collaboration.* You can improvise on stage, you can use an improv mindset to write a screenplay, or you can simply use improv as a way to be present. Despite the raging debate between process and product, improv can exist as both a tool for creating *and* as a means of performance. Its implementation in both ways has made improvisation one of the most important forms of contemporary performance.

While it is popular to celebrate the unlimited freedom of improv, in reality, like most modes of performance, it is usually most effective within set parameters. As Jeanne Leep outlines in *Theatrical Improvisation*, there are three main forms of improv that allow players focused freedom: *short form, long form, and sketch-based improv.* They all share several common theories, such as agreement, "Yes, And", etc. (explored more fully in Section II), but they also have sharp divisions both theoretically and in performance. Developed in part from the theater games of Viola Spolin and Keith Johnstone, short form improv has become the "pop" version of improv – the most widespread genre of improvisation both onstage and onscreen. It is usually shorter in nature and heavily reliant on games and gimmicks to propel the action forward. The television show *Whose Line Is It Anyway?* as well as ComedySportz and Theatresports are the most widely known examples of short form improv.

4

Long form is based on scenes and relationships and more closely resembles a one-act play (or an episode of *Seinfeld*, *30 Rock* … or pretty much any comedy on television right now). Long form doesn't mean that each scene is long (and boring), it means that instead of a string of independent games, the entire performance is interconnected. Long form is the most popular style at many of the leading improv theaters, including iO and the Upright Citizens Brigade. Sketch is written work based on or derived from improvisation, often referred to as sketch comedy, such as the performance work done at The Second City, The Brave New Workshop, The Groundlings, and to an extent on *Saturday Night Live*.

So now that we have an idea about what improv is, let's look at how we got to where we are now. History time! The following section gives a basic overview of contemporary improv by looking at the major theaters, and several of the major titans of improvisation. You need to know these theaters and these people because they created what you are doing; one day you might be performing at one of these theaters and it's always handy to know a little bit about your workplace.

Suggestions for Further Reading

Jeanne Leep's *Theatrical Improvisation: Short Form, Long Form, and Sketch-Based Improv*

Keith Johnstone's *Impro: Improvisation for the Theatre*

Mick Napier's *Improvise: Scene from the Inside Out*

Charna Halpern, Del Close, and Kim "Howard" Johnson's *Truth in Comedy*

Matt Besser, Ian Roberts, and Matt Walsh's *The Upright Citizens Brigade Comedy Improvisation Manual*

Mary Scruggs and Michael Gellman's *Process: An Improviser's Journey*

Kelly Leonard and Tom Yorton's *Yes, And: How Improvisation Reverses "No, But" Thinking and Improves Creativity and Collaboration—Lessons from The Second City*

Matt Fotis's *Long Form Improvisation and American Comedy: The Harold* (*NOTE: I will recommend this book for everything. Even if it isn't listed, just assume that it is. Please buy it. I have three kids to feed.)

Laura Numeroff's *If You Give a Mouse a Cookie* (or any book in that series). Yes, this is a children's book. It is also a great example of "Yes, And", Making Active Choices, Progressing the Story, Reincorporation, and The End is in the Beginning.

Notes

1 Amy Seham. *Whose Improv Is It Anyway?* Jackson, MS: University Press of Mississippi, 2001, xvii.
2 Mick Napier. *Improvise: Scene From the Inside Out.* Portsmouth, NH: Heinemann, 2004, 1.

6

Improv History

Commedia Dell'arte

Improv is literally as old as language, with most every society and civilization using improvisation as a form of communication. The most direct ancestor of contemporary improvisational theater, however, is *commedia dell'arte*, which emerged in Italy in the sixteenth century, eventually branching out to most of Europe before virtually disappearing from the mainstream in the eighteenth century.

Commedia troupes consisted of approximately six to ten performers that traveled from town to town performing improvised scenarios.

These scenarios were written by members of the company and usually consisted of a basic plot outline but contained no dialogue. During the performance the actors invented the words[1] and actions to get from plot point to plot point as they went along. This simple formula, later known as a scenario play, would provide a blueprint for The Compass Players to follow in the 1950s. In fact, scripted scenarios with no set dialogue have historically been the most prevalent style of performance in popular entertainment.

While the dialogue was spontaneous, much of *commedia dell'arte*'s success came from its reliance on popular scenarios and stock characters. Characters were broken into three categories: Masters, Servants, and Aristocrats (or non-masked characters). The masters include Magnifico, the leader of the city/town; Pantalone, the miserly, greedy, egotistical merchant (who often also merged with Magnifico into one character); and Dottore, the scholarly fool who knows everything about everything (but of course knows nothing of any practical value), who often argues and bickers with Pantalone. The servants are headed by Columbina, the servant girl who is smart, cunning, moral, and beautiful; Brighella, the self-serving, cunning top servant; Harlequin, the comic servant; and Zanni, who was usually Magnifico's servant, an enthusiastic, naïve, and curious peasant fresh to the city.

The Aristocrats include the 1st Actor and Actress, who don't wear masks and are usually of middle age, and the 2nd Actor and Actress, who also don't wear masks and are the young lovers, often the children of Pantalone and Dottore. Il Capitano, the foreign braggart soldier who would rather do anything than actually fight, is the other major character. A typical plot followed the two young lovers who were forbid to marry by the parents. Pantolone wants his daughter to marry the older and more successful (at least on the surface) Il Capitano. Through the help of the Servants, the two young lovers are able to convince Pantalone that they should be together and everyone gets what they deserve.

In addition to a fairly standard plot, a *commedia* actor was aided by the fact that he or she typically only played one character throughout his or her career. Most importantly, however, a *commedia* performer was reliant on the practice of employing standard *lazzi*, or what we would now call bits, which consist of any independent, comic, and repeatable activity that guaranteed laughs for its participants. The Upright Citizens Brigade's "the game of the scene" is really derived from *lazzi* – any repeatable action the performers use and exploit to get laughs and progress the scene.

Commedia dell'arte created an entirely new brand of theater reliant on the radical notion of improvised dialogue that ultimately transformed the comic theater. Its plots and characters have been used time and again from Shakespeare to modern-day Hollywood. Physical comics such as Charlie Chaplin, The Marx Brothers, The Three Stooges, and Lucille Ball owe *commedia dell'arte* a debt of gratitude. Even the famous routines of Abbott and Costello harken to the *lazzi* of *commedia dell'arte*. And of course, the scenario play format would help revolutionize comedy in the twentieth century.

Suggestions for Further Reading

John Rudlin's *Commedia Dell'Arte: An Actor's Handbook*

Mel Gordon's *Lazzi: The Comic Routines of the Commedia dell'Arte*

The National Theatre has a great set of short videos about *commedia* led by Didi Hopkins: http://www.nationaltheatre.org.uk/backstage/commedia-dellarte

9

Vaudeville and Burlesque

Originating in the nineteenth century, vaudeville and burlesque became the most important means of comedic performance during the first half of the twentieth century. Vaudeville performances were essentially variety shows consisting of unconnected musical, dance, comedy, and specialty acts. Burlesque performances were similar, but featured comic parodies, and of course, dancing women. The comic routines in vaudeville and burlesque were similar, though the latter were often much raunchier and blue – double entendre humor and adultery scenes were particular favorites, while vaudeville acts were marked by their "cleanness." It's sort of like an HBO comedy series (burlesque) versus a network television sitcom (vaudeville).

Much like *commedia*, which was a huge influence on both performance styles, the two forms celebrated improvisation. Most of the comedic bits and sketches in vaudeville and burlesque were passed down through an oral tradition. Unlike today, comedians didn't sit around writing new material during the day and then trying it out at night – there wasn't really any concern about authorship because the material was part of a shared tradition. Most of the bits and sketches were stock material that had been around for decades. The bits were simply scenarios – estimates range from anywhere between 400 and 15,000 standard bits. A comic or straight man was expected to know the bits and be able to step into any performance without rehearsing. Comics would repeat these bits, adding in their own jokes, or modifying the bit for their own purposes. Much like *commedia*'s scenario plays, the basic outline for a bit was fairly generic; it was the way performers personalized the bit that made it unique and funny.

Unlike contemporary improvisation where players create the material on the spot, improvisation in vaudeville and burlesque was used as a way for performers to personalize the material. Celebrated vaudeville performers Abbott & Costello, the most famous comedic duo of the 1940s and 50s (and quite possibly still the most famous comic duo), are best known for their classic sketch "Who's On First" … only it wasn't written by the duo. It was adapted from a variety of sources that played on a similar misunderstanding due to names. The duo wasn't the only one to perform the bit either, though because they performed the bit on radio and then later on television, authorship has been attributed to them. Bud Abbott claimed to have never memorized the bit and said that they never performed it the same way twice. He speaks of it as a living organic being that could be changed and adapted during performance – the pair often tried to catch one another off guard during the bit, keeping it fresh and spontaneous.

Not only was improv used to keep material fresh and unique, but due to the performance burden of vaudeville and burlesque, improvisation was a means to create – or more aptly, to adapt – material in a relatively quick manner. Burlesque and vaudeville had in some instances a nearly constant performance schedule. Performers either traveled on the circuit performing in different cities every night or week, up to 40 weeks a year, or were performing two or three shows a day over the course of a 12-hour "continuous" performance. As such, performers hardly had time to sit back and write new material since they were almost always on stage or backstage. Therefore they used the stage as a means to create/adapt material.

With the advent of radio and later television, burlesque and vaudeville disappeared from the stage. The improvisatory spirit carried on into early radio and television comedy, where performers often eschewed scripts in favor of improvisatory bits. There were usually scripts and stories present, but much like their time on the

10

stage, performers often inserted their own bits or jokes. This style of working can be seen today in contemporary comedic filmmaking in the films of Adam McKay, Judd Apatow, and Paul Feig among many others, where improvisation is used throughout the writing and filming process.

Nearly all of the twentieth century's earliest comedians were trained in vaudeville and burlesque. Its bits and sketches have been repeated for over a century, and its influence on contemporary comedy is hard to measure. From the basic straight man and comic duo that can be seen in virtually every buddy-cop/lawyer/detective/friend/etc. movie of the last 50 years to the repetition of jokes to the comic rhythm of performers like Abbott & Costello to the improvisational spirit of performance, vaudeville and burlesque have had a profound impact on American comedy and improvisational theater.

Suggestions for Further Reading

Andrew Davis's *Baggy Pants Comedy: Burlesque and the Oral Tradition*

Douglas Gilbert's *American Vaudeville: Its Life and Times*

Go watch Abbott & Costello's "Who's on First?"

Viola Spolin (1906–94)

Viola Spolin wanted to be an actress. It didn't work out. So instead she developed a system of theater games that revolutionized American comedy. The "High Priestess of Improv," Spolin remains to this day the single biggest influence on improvisational theater.

Spolin's comedic revolution is rooted in her work as a social worker at Hull House, a settlement house in Chicago founded by Jane Addams. She was heavily influenced by her training in the 1920s with Northwestern University sociologist Neva L. Boyd, who believed that play was essential to the human spirit, teaching life skills such as social adaptability, mental and emotional control, the ability to adjust to changing circumstances, and imagination. Spolin took her experience with Boyd and put it into practice when she became the drama supervisor for the Works Progress Administration's Recreation Project in Chicago (1939–41).

What Spolin created at the WPA and later with the Young Actors Company in Hollywood was a base of theater games, collectively known later as the "Theater Games" system of actor training, and published in 1963's *Improvisation for the Theater*. The system transformed complicated dramatic techniques and conventions into a series of games focused on spontaneity, physicality, intuition, and imagination that were designed to make play the catalyst for creativity, self-expression, and self-awareness.

As if inventing a new form of theatrical training and performance wasn't enough, she also trained the actors for a revolutionary new theater, The Compass Players, which would change the face of a city and the course of American comedy.

Suggestions for Further Reading

Viola Spolin's *Improvisation for the Theater*

Viola Spolin's *Theater Games for the Classroom: A Teacher's Handbook*

Viola Spolin and Paul Sills's *Theater Games for the Lone Actor*

Or make your way to Northwestern University Library and visit the Viola Spolin Papers.

12

The Compass Players

In the summer of 1955, The Compass Players opened in a storefront connected to a bar in Chicago's Hyde Park, near the University of Chicago. Initially intended to be a politically charged Brechtian cabaret that reflected the struggle of the workingman, the company quickly began to perform a variety of improvised performances and sketches that would change the landscape of American comedy.

David Shepherd,[2] one of improv's true pioneers, came to Chicago to start a new type of theater that spoke to the concerns of the common man (and also created the typical improv cabaret/bar-type setup that can be found at pretty much every improv theater in America). A wealthy New York aristocrat who had become bored and troubled by the bourgeois plays of Broadway, Shepherd wanted to use the scenario play format from *commedia dell'arte* to create up-to-the-minute plays that were relevant to the concerns of the masses, reflecting their problems and presented in an accessible style. Needing someone able to work with improvisation and train actors to portray these new plays, Shepherd turned to director (and Viola Spolin's son) Paul Sills. Using improvisation as a means to create these scenarios, Sills, along with Spolin for a short time, trained the company in this new style of performance.

Initially the group presented these improvised scenario plays, but legend has it that bartender Fred Wranovics asked if they could make the show longer so he could sell another round of drinks. The actors, not having any more material prepared to fill this desired time slot, and growing weary from the demanding nature of constantly creating new scenario plays, seized on the idea of creating material based on audience suggestions. Actors and audience members alike became more attracted to the improvised portion of the show. The actors quickly began writing, rehearsing, and polishing these improvised scenes into sketches that were subsequently performed, most notably the routines of Mike Nichols and Elaine May. The group developed other performance forms that likewise became more popular than the scenario plays, including the highly influential Living Newspaper, which was derived from the Living Newspaper segments from The Federal Theater Project. In The Compass version, which usually opened the show, players would read the newspaper and then begin satirizing stories/items through quick pantomimed scenes or spoken word bits. In much the same way that *The Daily Show* and other contemporary "fake news" shows satirize the news, The Compass aimed to show audiences the mechanics, biases, absurdity, and inner workings of the news.

In part due to artistic divides within the group – Shepherd wanted more politically charged scenario plays, while Sills and most of the actors (and audiences) wanted more sketches and improv – as well as an ill-fated move to a more traditional theater space on the north side of Chicago, the group disbanded in 1957. Later that year a second branch was opened in St. Louis under the direction of Ted Flicker, featuring several members from the Chicago branch, as well as the talents of a former fire-eating circus performer named Del Close. The St. Louis branch presented a more polished form of improvisation fueled by Flicker's louder, faster, funnier approach. The meandering and lengthy improvised scenes of Chicago were turned into short, powerful, focused scenes in St. Louis. Playful and poignant, the scenes were presented in a sort of carnivalesque manner, with Flicker acting as ringmaster. Flicker realized that if improv was to succeed as an art form, it needed to transform itself, and he did that by making improv the product. Much like its Chicago predecessor, the St. Louis branch had a relatively short life. But both companies would live on, with the St. Louis company planting the seeds of what later became long form improvisation and ultimately iO, and with The Second City growing out of the ashes of the Chicago Compass.

Suggestions for Further Reading

Janet Coleman's *The Compass: The Improvisational Theatre that Revolutionized American Comedy*

Jeffrey Sweet's *Something Wonderful Right Away: An Oral History of The Second City and The Compass Players*

Go watch Nichols and May's "Mother & Son" sketch (sometimes this is called "Telephone" or "Mother & Son Telephone" or "A Mother's Prayer" or some version of that name … it doesn't matter if you find the right one, just go watch (or listen to) some Nichols and May).

Then go watch the documentary *Compass Cabaret 55* by Mark Siska.

The Second City

From the ashes of The Compass Players,[3] Paul Sills, Bernard Sahlins, and Howard Alk founded arguably the most influential American theater of the twentieth century. Opening its doors on December 16, 1959, on North Wells Street in Chicago in what had been a Chinese laundry, The Second City ushered in the age of irony, satire, and sketch comedy. Building upon the ideas Sills and others explored with The Compass, The Second City developed a system of sketch comedy derived from improvisation that satirized the social, cultural, and political issues of the day.

Instead of using a plot outline to create plays, The Second City began writing down successful sketches and compiling them into what are known as sketch revues. According to Second City producer Bernard Sahlins, a revue is "a stage presentation that uses short scenes of varying lengths. Add music and songs and think of it as generally comical and topical by nature."[4] The basic format for a Second City revue is a combination between a play and a collage of scenes. Usually existing in two acts and running between 90 minutes and 2 hours, the revue is made up of several types of scenes: blackouts, parodies, songs, relating scenes, satires, and improvised games. Usually built around an overarching theme or topic, revues often take pointed jabs at social, political, and cultural norms by turning mainstream ideas about religion, race, politics, and culture on their head.

Behind this new type of socially relevant and subversive comedy Second City was immediately successful, so much so that they had to quickly move to a larger space on Wells Street to accommodate the growing crowds. The theater also began attracting throngs of young comedians looking to make it onto The Second City stage. Seeing the opportunity for an ever-present talent pool, Second City began training improvisers. The first improv workshops were held in 1960, were then refined over the next decade, and in 1971 Jo Forsberg founded The Players Workshop, which was the unofficial school for the theater until 1985 when The Second City Training Center opened under the leadership of Martin de Maat. Initially students had to finish at The Players Workshop before being admitted to The Second City Training Center. Second City would become the Harvard of improv schools, seen as *the* place to study improv, but always espousing the paradoxical message of being an improv theater that did scripted work. The résumés of their graduates and the sheer number of famous alumni, unparalleled by any training school, certainly attests to the theater's results.

A touring company was created in 1967 that performed "Best of Second City" shows across North America, and Second City satellites were also founded in Toronto, Detroit, Las Vegas, Los Angeles, and many other cities (most flourished but a few did not). The most important of these satellites was the Toronto branch, which opened in 1973. The Toronto Second City featured among its cast Dan Aykroyd, Eugene Levy, John Candy, and Gilda Radner. The troupe, under the auspices of Second City Toronto owner Andrew Alexander, who would later take over the Chicago branch with Len Stuart in 1985 when Bernie Sahlins left the theater, would also launch the successful and influential television show *SCTV* in 1976 on the heels of another revolutionary comedic television show. In 1975, the Toronto and Chicago branches became, and continue to be, the talent foundation for *Saturday Night Live*, a show that would change the face of American comedy to look an awful lot like Second City's. Aside from its role as a talent pipeline for *SNL*, Second City continues to this day to be the most abundant source of new comedic talent in North America.

Second City's impact on improv is so vast that it is difficult to overestimate its importance; it vaulted improvisational theater, ironically through scripted sketch comedy, into the spotlight of American comedy.

15

Suggestions for Further Reading

Anne Libera's *The Second City Almanac of Improvisation*

Sheldon Patinkin's *The Second City: Backstage at the World's Greatest Comedy Theater*

Bernard Sahlins's *Days and Nights at The Second City: A Memoir, with Notes on Staging Review Theatre*

Mike Thomas's *The Second City Unscripted: Revolution and Revelation at the World-Famous Comedy Theater*

Jeffrey Sweet's *Something Wonderful Right Away: An Oral History of the Second City and the Compass Players*

The Committee

A group of Second City alumni came to San Francisco for a summer and stayed for a decade. Founded by Alan and Jessica Myerson in 1963, The Committee was a sketch comedy theater that had a strong political bent. Initially performing in a former indoor bocce ball court, the company quickly became a staple of San Francisco's comedy and counter-culture scene, as well as becoming a strong force in Los Angeles in the late 1960s. Mirroring the cultural, political, and social climate of 1960s San Francisco, The Committee had a sharp satirical and political edge that pushed boundaries, featuring some of the first instances of drug humor, openly gay characters (that weren't a complete mockery), and cutting social and political satire. Along with sketch comedy that took direct aim at cultural norms, The Committee pioneered performance improvisation. They helped lay the groundwork for much of what would become long form improvisation, and created this little thing called the Harold.

While they created the Harold, it was not the Harold we know and love today. First performed in 1967, the early Harold was a free-flowing loosely collected collage that explored a theme and more closely resembled what we would call a Montage. Myerson, Del Close (who joined after the first of many partings from Second City), and the group envisioned a form that would introduce characters and themes that would then reappear throughout the performance with the collection of scenes washing over the audience. While the same concept still underpins the Harold, the early form had no real structure and frequently was nothing more than a collection of (sometimes) semi-related scenes. What the early Harold did that was different from other types of performance improv was to use the entire ensemble united in one performance that was (theoretically) connected, rather than isolated individual sketches, scenes, or games. Close would take this Harold with him when he returned to Chicago where, when he teamed up with Charna Halpern in the early 1980s, they'd transform it into the Harold we know today.

During their decade-long stint, The Committee made numerous television appearances (the group regularly appeared on *The Dick Cavett Show*), recorded three studio albums, and were hugely influential in the development of American comedy, with alumni spreading out across California and the US. Del Close of course famously took the Harold to Chicago, while Gary Austin went to Los Angeles where he formed The Groundlings. Other alums went on to successful careers in television and film, working on projects like *WKRP in Cincinnati*, *The Smothers Brothers Comedy Hour*, *Jaws*, *The Jerk*, and *This is Spinal Tap*.

Suggestions for Further Reading   17

There shockingly isn't a book about The Committee (yet). So maybe you can go write it. Or you can go fund the documentary *The Committee: A Secret History of American Comedy* … or if it's already out, go watch it.

The Groundlings

Los Angeles's oldest improv and sketch comedy company (and school), The Groundlings began in 1972 as The Gary Austin Workshop. Austin, who was a member of the famed San Francisco group The Committee (which also featured Del Close and first created the Harold), simply wanted to gather improvisers to work on their craft. In 1974 the group was formally founded and named The Groundlings after the audience members who stood in front of the stage to watch Shakespearean theater. The company originally developed material during weekday workshops and performed the best material on the weekend, and has grown to where they now produce four fully realized sketch comedy revues a year, referred to as the Main Shows, along with a variety of alternative comedy productions.

Initially the group was roughly a dozen performers and shows were held in a 30-seat basement theater. Despite these humble beginnings, buzz quickly grew around the company. Lily Tomlin regularly attended early performances and hired several Groundlings to perform on *The Lily Tomlin Show*. Lorne Michaels and *Saturday Night Live* also began taking notice, hiring Laraine Newman to be one of the early cast members, starting a long-standing pipeline between The Groundlings and *SNL* that includes Will Ferrell, Phil Hartman, Jon Lovitz, Julia Sweeney, Cheri Oteri, Chris Kattan, Ana Gasteyer, Chris Parnell, Maya Rudolph, Will Forte, and Kristen Wiig.

The group grew exponentially and moved to a permanent home in 1979 (they secured the space in 1975 but for a variety of reasons didn't open the space for four years). That same year Austin stepped down as artistic director, replaced by Tom Maxwell, who would hold the post for ten years. In 1989, The Main Company collectively took over as artistic director, with each new revue directed by a current member or alum. The training school also began in 1979, and in 1982 The Sunday Company was formed by Suzanne Kent to further develop promising students. After working with The Sunday Company, performers become eligible to be voted into the Main Company. Several notable alumni came through The Sunday Company, including Conan O'Brien, Jimmy Fallon, Rita Wilson, Darryl Hannah, and Nasim Pedrad.

Along with the Main Shows the company began producing alternative shows, including Paul Rubens's *The Pee Wee Herman Show*. In 1992, Melanie Graham created "Cooking With Gas," a weekly short form improv show featuring members of the Main Company, Sunday Company, and celebrity guests, which became the longest-running improv show in Los Angeles.

Still operating today, The Groundlings remains one of the premiere comedy theaters in the country. While iO West and UCB West have recently been established in LA, The Groundlings remains at the city's comedic forefront.

Loose Moose Theatre Company

While Second City opened a Toronto branch that would become one of the most influential theaters in the world, over in Calgary in 1977 Keith Johnstone and Mel Tonken founded the Loose Moose Theatre Company. Based on Johnstone's teachings (see below for more info on Johnstone), the group has become a premiere training and performance ground, most famous for Theatresports.

Theatresports is the most widespread form of improv to originate at the Loose Moose, though it is now licensed through the International Theatresports Institute. Based on Johnstone's theories of improvisation, the basic format features two teams competing in improv games and stories for points. While ComedySportz uses a similar format (see below for more on CS), their shows tend to focus more on the competitive aspect and feature more gags and jokes, whereas Theatresports focuses more on collaborative improvised storytelling.

The theater continues to operate, and hosts a two-week summer International Improvisation School (more info in the Professional Training Section) that brings together improvisers and Theatresports practitioners from around the world.

Suggestions for Further Reading

Keith Johnstone's *Impro: Improvisation for the Theatre*

Keith Johnstone's *Impro for Storytellers*

Theresa Robbins Dudeck's *Keith Johnstone: A Critical Biography*

19

Keith Johnstone (1933–)

A legendary teacher, playwright, and director, Keith Johnstone is one of the pioneers of improvisational theater. He's widely known for creating the Theatresports style of improv, as well as his two books on improvisational theater, *Impro* and *Impro for Storytellers*. He worked as a playwright with the Royal Court Theatre in London and created and toured with the Theatre Machine Improvisation group in England, before moving to Calgary in 1970, where he co-founded the Loose Moose Theatre in 1977 where he fully developed the Impro training system.

Born and raised in England, Johnstone found the public school system deplorable. He felt that it stymied his imagination and creativity, and worked to actively make him shy and self-conscious. His teachings, which began at the Royal Court Theatre in London, are based on the complete opposite approach. Instead of viewing children as immature adults that needed scolding and standardization to be molded into responsible grown-ups, he viewed adults as atrophied children who had lost their sense of imagination and play. He wanted to create spontaneous, creative, and open actors by tapping into the latent creativity and spontaneity inside everyone. Rather than trying to be someone or something else, Johnstone's teachings center on being true to your own unique individual self and trusting your own instincts and ideas.

Laid out in detail in *Impro*, the basic concept involves playing games to become more free and spontaneous. He's famous for urging students to not prepare and to dare to be average. His concept of originality is based on simply being true to yourself and your instincts rather than trying to create something you think the teacher wants. Some of his favorite maxims include: "You can't learn anything without failing." "Please don't do your best. Trying to do your best is trying to be better than you are." "Go onto stage to make relationships. At least you won't be alone." Johnstone is one of improv's legendary teachers, coining many of the basic philosophies we use in classes today, including introducing the ideas of reincorporation and status, both of which are further explored in Section II.

In 1998 he founded the International Theatresports Institute, which joins together the many Theatresports companies throughout the world.

20

Suggestions for Further Reading

Keith Johnstone's *Impro: Improvisation for the Theatre*

Keith Johnstone's *Impro for Storytellers*

Theresa Robbins Dudeck's *Keith Johnstone: A Critical Biography*

iO

The Second City created a comedy empire by using improvisation to write sketch comedy. A growing number of improvisers, led by Del Close, sought to make improv the main attraction. Founded in 1981 by David Shepherd, his second attempt at a populist theater, ImprovOlympic[5] sought to make improv the product. Shepherd quickly brought in Charna Halpern to help run the theater. They wanted the focus to be on the audience, and one of the ways Shepherd sought to do this was through a competitive format called The

Improvisational Olympiad. In his new populist theater, two teams of improvisers would compete in a series of ten distinct improv games with the audience picking the winner at the end of the night. Each performance would feature one professional team made up of improvisers with previous experience or training, and a team of amateurs with no improv experience like The God Squad, which was a team of rabbis. While the theater had moderate success, Halpern quickly grew tired of the format, and Shepherd left the company.

As luck would have it, in 1983 Second City had just parted ways (again) with its recalcitrant resident director Del Close. Halpern knew that improv had more to offer, and like everyone in Chicago had heard the legends about Close. Thinking he'd make an ideal partner, Halpern offered Close $200 and some pot to teach a class on whatever he wanted. After the class Halpern was floored and took Close out for coffee, again telling him that she was looking for something more out of improv. He mentioned he had a form he'd been working on for years called the Harold, and told her that if she closed her little game theater he would come teach at ImprovOlympic. Halpern and Close set to work structuring the Harold, and reopened ImprovOlympic on October 1, 1984 totally rebranded as the first exclusively long form improv theater in the world.

Explored more fully in Section V, the Harold is a long form structure that takes three distinctly separate scenes and over the course of a half-hour combines the characters, themes, and situations in unique and interesting ways. The humor arises from the relationships, connections, and callbacks, rather than from jokes or games. Behind the Harold iO ushered in a new style of ensemble-based comedy: what Close called slow comedy. He wanted players to take their time, to break the joke-based rhythm of comedy. He wanted players to wait for the third thought, rather than simply respond with the first. For Close, the first thought would be a knee-jerk reaction, whereas the third thought would bring more truth, depth, honesty, and ultimately, humor to a scene.

Slow comedy is at the core of iO's training center, one of the premiere comedy schools in the country, and is the basis for Close, Halpern, and Kim "Howard" Johnson's *Truth in Comedy* (1994). Many of today's most successful comedians, including Chris Farley, Tim Meadows, Mike Meyers, Adam McKay, Tina Fey, and Amy Poehler, initially trained at iO.

Charna Halpern, Del Close, and Kim "Howard" Johnson's *Truth in Comedy*

Matt Fotis's *Long Form Improvisation and American Comedy: The Harold*

Del Close (1934–99)

Del Close was an actor, writer, stand-up, author, "mad scientist," and teacher who revolutionized improvisational comedy. Known to many as "the guru," Close is the (co)-father of the Harold and helped create an improv style not based on games but on scenic relationships, honesty, and connections. He dedicated his life to proving that improv was more than a tool for sketch comedy – that it was in fact a viable means of performance in its own right.

Close began his improv career in the late 1950s with the St. Louis Compass Players. While there, he was introduced to the major concepts of improvisation, and along with Ted Flicker and Elaine May helped establish the first set of rules for improv. In 1960 Close moved to Chicago, his home base for much of the rest of his life. He initially worked at The Second City, but was fired (numerous times) due to substance abuse and things like not showing up to work. He spent the latter half of the 1960s in San Francisco where he worked with The Committee, the first group to perform a Harold, and created light images for Grateful Dead shows. In 1972 he returned to Chicago, and to Second City, serving as resident director for the next ten years.

Over the next decade he trained many popular comedians, including a stint in the early 1980s as "house metaphysician" at *Saturday Night Live*. At *SNL* and beyond, Close's students and protégés were becoming household names, and crediting "the guru" with their success. Close spent the mid-to-late 1980s and 1990s teaching at ImprovOlympic. His decades-long drug and substance abuse, however, caught up to him and Close died on March 4, 1999, five days before his 65th birthday. In his will he bequeathed his skull to the Goodman Theater to be used in its productions of *Hamlet*. His will specified that he be duly credited in the program as portraying Yorick and that when he was not "performing" it be put on display. Although Charna Halpern stood by her story that the skull donated was indeed Close's, she later admitted in a *New Yorker* interview that the skull given to the theater was not his but in fact a purchased skull from a local medical supply company.

Skull or no skull, Del Close's legacy cannot be overstated. His basic rules of agreeing to the reality of the scene, making active choices, and wearing a character as a thin veil have become so well respected that they are the basis for almost all improvisation. The popularity and influence of the Harold can be seen beyond iO in contemporary film and television. Close's drive and persistence allowed him to create a new generation of improvisers, claiming that improvisation, in itself, is an art form and not just the means to an end.

Suggestions for Further Reading

Charna Halpern, Del Close, and Kim "Howard" Johnson's *Truth in Comedy*

Kim "Howard" Johnson's *The Funniest One in the Room: The Lives and Legends of Del Close*

Jeff Griggs's *Guru: My Days with Del Close*

Matt Fotis's *Long Form Improvisation and American Comedy: The Harold*   23

ComedySportz

ComedySportz is an improvisational comedy chain started in 1984 in Milwaukee, Wisconsin, by a group of local comedians including Dick Chudnow. Based on the competitive Theatresports improvisational techniques of Keith Johnstone, ComedySportz is the premiere short form improv theater in America with over 20 theaters around the country.

The traditional format of a ComedySportz show features two teams of improvisational performers competing in various short form improv games with audience members judging the results and awarding points (and sometimes joining the players on stage). A ComedySportz match features two teams competing for laughs and points, with a referee keeping things fast and clean. An average of seven to twelve games are played during a match, drawn from a repertoire of over a hundred improv games. For example, in "Shakespeare" a team will improvise a scene inspired by an audience suggestion in Shakespearian style. In "Forward/Reverse" the referee sends the scene back and forth at will, as though scanning a scene in a DVD, sending the players into a frenzy. Every show is different, with different players, different games, and different audiences supplying new suggestions. The fans judge the scenes and games and ultimately decide the winners and losers.

In every show, a ComedySportz referee monitors the action, awarding points and administering fouls as necessary. Much like the television show *Whose Line Is It Anyway?*, ComedySportz is a high-energy mass-produced form of entertainment. The audience of a typical ComedySportz match contains everyone from kids to college students to parents and grandparents. There is a distinct mass-appeal approach, so much so that the referee calls fouls on players to keep the comedy clean. Two of ComedySportz's most widely called penalties are the Brown Bag Foul and the Groaner Foul. A Brown Bag Foul is called when a performer uses explicit language or refers to something crass or off-color. The offender must wear a brown paper bag over his or her head for the remainder of the scene, even if the offender is an audience member. A Groaner Foul is called when a performer tells a pun bad enough to make the audience groan. The player loses at least one point for his or her team, unless his or her apology to the audience is heartfelt enough.

Suggestions for Further Reading

Amy Seham's *Whose Improv Is It Anyway? Beyond Second City*

The Comedy Store Players

The Comedy Store Players, performing at the famed Comedy Store in London, is one of Europe's most influential short form improv groups. The Comedy Store Players started in 1985, performing the second act of a show that started with stand-up comedy – they thought nobody would come to only see improv (reportedly only 20 people showed up that night anyway). Three decades later the Comedy Store Players have proven to be one of the most successful improv groups ever.

Original members Mike Meyers and Kit Hollerbach taught the improv games they had been playing in America and Canada, mostly inspired by Viola Spolin. The group quickly began to develop their own style, though continue to perform mostly short form improv games. With the popularity of *Whose Line Is It Anyway?*, the group suddenly became a hot ticket, with many cast members regularly

24

appearing on the television program. The group added a Wednesday evening performance to their regular Sunday performance, and as has been the norm since, both shows began selling out.

Unlike almost every other improv group or theater, The Comedy Store Players have maintained essentially the same cast for over 25 years. While Meyers left in 1986, the core of Neil Mullarkey, Paul Merton, Josie Lawrence, Lee Simpson, Andy Smart, Jim Sweeney, and Richard Vranch have been working together for decades. This longevity is unheard of in improv, where teams and players often shift or disappear on a monthly basis. In 2010 the group entered the Guinness World Record book as the longest-running comedy show with the same cast. Though there were of course some additions and subtractions, the core cast has been relatively stable for over two decades.

Suggestions for Further Reading

William Cook's *The Comedy Store: The Club that Changed British Comedy*

Whose Line Is It Anyway?

Whose Line Is It Anyway? is a short form improvisational comedy show created by Dan Patterson and Mark Leveson. Originally a British radio program, it moved to television in 1988 for a ten-season run, featuring many of The Comedy Store Players. Following the conclusion of the British run in 1998, ABC began airing an American version consisting of Drew Carey as host, Wayne Brady, Colin Mochrie, Ryan Stiles, and a fourth guest as performers.

The show consists of a panel of four short form performers who create characters, scenes, and songs on the spot. Topics for the games are based on either audience suggestions or predetermined prompts from the host. Both the British and American shows take the form of a game show with the host arbitrarily assigning points and choosing a "winner" at the end of each episode. The points, however, "don't really matter" and simply allow the host and performers an extra comedic outlet. At the conclusion of each episode, the host chooses a winner or several winners arbitrarily. The "prize" for winning on the British version of the show was to read the credits in a certain style, chosen by the host, as they scrolled. On the American series, the "prize" was either to play a game with the host, or to sit out while the other performers did.

One of the hallmarks of the show, especially the American version, was the way that it highlighted its performers. While most improv is about ensemble, *Whose Line* was very much about the individual performers – their strengths (and sometimes their weaknesses). While the performers certainly worked together, the show was often more of an outlet for the performers' individual talents – e.g. Wayne Brady singing in pretty much every episode. The show's mass appeal on two continents and relatively long life has made it the point of entry for most improv audience members and performers. As such, its influence on contemporary improvisation is vast, with many groups using the show as their main source of inspiration.

The Annoyance

With the establishment of the Harold at iO, a codified short form structure at ComedySportz, and the successful formula of *Whose Line* on television, improvisation finally had firm structures that allowed for a fairly reliable end product. So naturally it didn't take long for a group to come along to break all the rules.

The Annoyance got its start at Indiana University in the early 1980s, when Mick Napier and David MacNerland formed the improv group Dubbletaque, having never seen or performed improv. The group used a Second City model – Napier had seen a grand total of one Second City revue – and created a brand new one-hour sketch show every week. Upon graduation Napier moved to Chicago to study improvisation, performing wherever he could, including on the ImprovOlympic Harold team Grime and Punishment. Napier, however, quickly grew weary of ImprovOlympic's sacrosanct view of the Harold. He felt like there was more to improv than just one form. Napier's wariness about the "truth" of the Harold and the rigid structure of ImprovOlympic helped form his philosophy of uncensored play, and was the guiding force behind the formation of his new company.

Founded in 1987 as Metraform (after some late-night soul-searching and a bottle of tequila, renamed The Annoyance Theatre), the company quickly established itself as the leading alternative improvisational theater in Chicago. After students trained at iO and Second City to learn the rules of improv, they came to The Annoyance to learn how to break those rules. Driven by the idea of unrestricted improvisation based in play, The Annoyance developed an irreverent performance philosophy, which as Rob Kozlowski notes in *The Art of Chicago Improv*, can be summed up in two words: "fuck it." Marrying a subversive style and a free-play mindset, The Annoyance defined itself with shows like *The Real Live Brady Bunch* (1990); *Manson: The Musical* (1990); *Tippi: Portrait of a Virgin* (1991); *Ayn Rand Gives Me a Boner* (1991); *What Every Girl Should Know—An Ode to Judy Blume* (1998); and their flagship show *Co-Ed Prison Sluts* (1989), one of the longest-running shows in Chicago musical theater history. The theater's calling card became subversion, whether it was rules, traditions, or simply good taste.

With a commitment to unrestricted creativity, coupled with a desire to have as many original shows playing simultaneously as possible, the group became a breeding ground for a new type of improvisational performance – full-length plays and musicals derived from improvisation. Convinced that improv would flourish in a safe environment void of improv rules that they felt handicapped improvisers on stage and focused more on improv as a commodity than anything else, The Annoyance has developed a hybrid model that allows for a blending of forms and styles. The Annoyance uses improv in whatever way serves the piece or performance best: as a tool, as a performance end, or as some combination of the two. Consequently, The Annoyance is known as much for its eclectic material as its trademark subversion, with as many as 13 different shows running in any one week. For them nothing is out of bounds, no topic too taboo, no structure or way of doing improv wrong. The only censorship comes from the artists themselves – if it fits the production then it stays, if it doesn't it goes.

Suggestions for Further Reading

Mick Napier's *Improvise: Scene from the Inside Out*

The Upright Citizens Brigade

If The Annoyance Theatre is the alternative to iO, established as a reaction against the Harold, in many ways the Upright Citizens Brigade is iO's bastard child. Founded in 1991 by a collection of iO improvisers and based on the teachings of Close and the Harold, the group relocated to New York in 1996 behind the UCB Four – Amy Poehler, Matt Besser, Matt Walsh, and Ian Roberts – bringing an absurd, aggressive, playful, and socially discontent brand of long form improv and the Harold with them. They entered a comedy scene that for several decades had been dominated by stand-up. Unlike Chicago, where long form improv had a long legacy and helped shape the city's comic aesthetic, in New York long form improvisation was virtually non-existent. The only major improv presence in New York at the time was Chicago City Limits, a short form-style theater. Filling a much-needed niche for collaborative ensemble-created improvised comedy, nearly two decades later the group has become one of the most influential comedy troupes in the country, with alumni flooding television and film.

Like many upstart groups, they initially had trouble attracting audiences, in part because they were doing something totally new. While the Harold formed their ideological base, their main performance form is ASSSSCAT, which is a monologue deconstruction based on The Armando Diaz – a form many of the UCB folks had performed at iO (Armando Diaz himself was an early member of UCB who went on to found The Magnet – see Section VII). The main difference between the form is that ASSSSCAT uses a guest monologist (Conan O'Brien was one such early guest) who tells personal stories that then inspire the very free-form and playful improvisation, instead of using a member of the troupe who more fully integrates the monologues into the show. The monologist often tells two or three separate stories, but the form can be done based on just one monologue. They began performing the form in Chicago, where the name originated as an homage to the form's deliberately sloppy and mess-around nature, and quickly became UCB's biggest draw when they relocated to New York. The form is still UCB's most popular show, featuring the theater's top performers and alumni. It has run continuously since 1996 and features a who's who of guest monologists.

In 1998 the *Upright Citizens Brigade*, a sketch show, aired on Comedy Central. It only ran until 2000, and while it wasn't improvised, it was structured much like a Harold with each show centered on a theme, with characters and themes weaving together in interesting and unexpected ways. They culled a majority of their material from past improv scenes and generated a greater part of their new material from the Sunday night ASSSSCAT performances, so it isn't surprising that the show felt like a Harold.

It was one of the first sketch shows since *SCTV* to revolve around a central theme and overarching narrative, rather than a loose collection of sketches about current events. The show was based around a fake group of "social terrorists" who sought to disrupt the status quo through sketch comedy. The show broke new ground for sketch comedy shows because it wasn't based on popular culture or celebrity impersonations, endlessly shoving catch-phrases down the audience's throat. Rather, like a Harold, the humor was based on connecting seemingly unrelated events, characters, and plots.

Suggestions for Further Reading

Matt Walsh, Ian Roberts, and Matt Besser's *Upright Citizens Brigade Comedy Improvisation Manual*

Brian Raftery's *High Status Characters: How the Upright Citizens Brigade Stormed a City, Started a Scene, and Changed Comedy Forever*

Improv Snapshots

While this book is mainly focused on American improvisational theater performed for comedic purposes, folks all around the globe use improv in a variety of ways. Improv is used as a training tool, such as with Anne Bogart's Viewpoints, Jerzy Grotowski's "poor theater," or even the Meisner Technique. It is used as a means of social action, such as with the many forms and incarnations of Interactive Theater and Forum Theater. These snapshots are meant to expose you to just a few of the ways improv works in the theater outside of comedy and to encourage you to dig deeper into the many ways improv is used and the many people who are using it.[6] For our purposes here, let's briefly look at three major non-American/non-comedic forms of improv – 1) Augusto Boal and the Theatre of the Oppressed, 2) Jacques Lecoq, and 3) J.L. Moreno's Psychodrama.

Augusto Boal (1931–2009) and the Theatre of the Oppressed

Boal was a Brazilian theater artist best known for his Theatre of the Oppressed (TO) form of improvisation. Using improv as a catalyst for social and political change, TO is a form of theater that uses the audience as an active participant – spect-actors – as they actively engage with, analyze, deconstruct, and ultimately transform their social and political reality.

Forum Theater is perhaps the most widespread of TO techniques. In a forum theater piece a set of actors will perform a short scene that involves some sort of oppression that is relevant to the audience. The players then replay the scene and the audience is encouraged to stop the action at any time and step into the situation and actively propose a solution. The audience isn't allowed to merely suggest things from their seats – they must actively become a participant in the action. The concept is that the spect-actor will not only face the challenges of overcoming the oppression, but that with the experience they will be more likely to take action in their real lives.

Image Theater is a TO technique in which one person becomes the sculptor and molds one or more actors/players into statues or images. The sculptor ideally avoids using language and instead uses touch to create the images. The idea is to remove language to get to the true meaning of a word through physical expression. For instance, the word "love" can mean many things, but an image will give all those present a concrete expression.

Invisible Theater is theater that exists in non-traditional theatrical spaces, such as in a store, restaurant, or simply in the streets. The players never give away that they are in fact performing, and instead attempt to present the performance as a real event. Onlookers may or may not intervene. Improv Everywhere is perhaps the best-known contemporary example of Invisible Theater.

Rainbow of Desire is a form of drama therapy that uses a series of techniques that tend to focus on internalized oppression in a single protagonist often against a single antagonist.

Suggestions for Further Reading

Augusto Boal's *Theatre of the Oppressed*

Augusto Boal's *Games for Actors and Non-Actors*

Augusto Boal's *The Rainbow of Desire: The Boal Method of Theatre and Therapy*

Jacques Lecoq (1921–99)

Regarded as one of the most influential teachers of the twentieth century, Jacques Lecoq is best known for his playful approach to physical theater. Influenced by *commedia dell'arte* as well as the mask work of Ancient Greek tragedy, Lecoq opened L'École Internationale de Théâtre in Paris in 1956. One of the leading schools of physical theater and acting, Lecoq's approach emphasizes a practical approach that is tailored to each specific actor focusing more on a performer's creativity than on a specific codified method. Lecoq believed that play was the most important element for a performer, noting that "There is a huge difference between actors who express their own lives, and those who can truly be described as players. ... They have learned not to play *themselves* but to play *using* themselves. In this lies all the ambiguity of the actor's work."[7] A performer's ability to play is prized above other skills.

A large component of Lecoq's approach relies on improvisation and mask work. Lecoq felt that improvisation helped reinforce the central role of play in performance, as well as allowing individuals to learn to express themselves and use their bodies. Mask work is also a huge component of Lecoq's philosophy. Lecoq believed that masks were a simple way to communicate ideas and emotions, as well as working to amplify the physical aspects of a performer. His work with masks, movement, and gesture has had a huge impact on contemporary theater.

Suggestions for Further Reading

Jacques Lecoq's *The Moving Body: Teaching Creative Theatre*

J.L. Moreno (1889–1974) and Psychodrama

J.L. Moreno (1889–1974) is known as "the man who brought laughter to psychiatry." He is best known for developing psychodrama, a method using psychotherapy where clients use spontaneous role-playing to gain insight into their lives. Similar to Boal's Rainbow of Desire, psychodrama works to recreate real-life situations so that clients have the chance to evaluate their choices/behavior and to more fully understand specific moments/incidents/situations in their lives.

Moreno believed that the best way to respond to a psychodrama situation is through spontaneity, or what he called "spontaneity-creativity." Based on his work in Europe where he began the Theatre of Spontaneity, psychodrama became his outlet for the power of spontaneity-creativity. He felt that a client would be best served by a willingness and readiness to improvise and respond spontaneously in the moment. Much like Forum Theater or Rainbow of Desire, Moreno believed that using spontaneous reactions would allow individuals to see problems in new ways and discover new solutions.

One central exercise to psychodrama is Mirroring. The protagonist acts out an experience, often with the help of the group. The protagonist then steps out of the scene and watches as another actor takes the role of protagonist and replays the scene. The client is then allowed to comment on the action and/or reenter the scene. Doubling is another major technique, where a second actor expresses any thoughts or feelings that the protagonist is unable to express. A third major technique is Role Reversal. Using this technique, the protagonist plays the part of another actor in the situation, while someone else portrays the protagonist.

Suggestions for Further Reading

David Read Johnson and Renee Emunah (eds) *Current Approaches in Drama Therapy*

Jonathan Moreno's *Impromptu Man: J.L. Moreno and the Origins of Psychodrama, Encounter Culture, and the Social Network*

Notes

1 Performers often spoke in a gibberish language known as Grammelot, which was a common "language" for physical comedy performance.
2 Shepherd continued experimenting with improvisational theater after The Compass. He would go on to co-found ImprovOlympic as well as the Canadian Improv Games. A recipient of lifetime achievement awards from the Chicago Improv Festival, Second City, and the Canadian Improv Games, Shepherd is one of the foundational icons of improvisation. The documentary *David Shepherd: A Lifetime of Improvisational Theatre* was released in 2010. His work and experiments have transformed the theater and the way we think about improvisation.
3 They wanted to reuse The Compass name, but Shepherd didn't want to be involved (and wasn't necessarily invited) and therefore didn't allow them to use the name. So Sills decided to turn the tables on A.J. Liebling's insulting reference to Chicago as the "second city," and changed the reference forever when he employed it as the name for his satirical theater.
4 Bernard Sahlins. *Days and Nights at the Second City*. Chicago: Ivan R. Dee, 2001, 115.
5 Originally named ImprovOlympics, the theater changed to ImprovOlympic in 1984 when it became a long form theater. In 2005, it became iO

because the U.S. Olympic Committee had sued the theater for fear that a small comedy theater would be confused with perhaps the largest international sporting event in the world.

6 For a more complete look at improv around the world, check out the rather exhaustive timeline in the appendix of David Alfred Charles's dissertation *The Novelty of Improvisation: Towards a Genre of Embodied Spontaneity.*

7 Jacques Lecoq. *The Moving Body: Teaching Creative Theatre.* New York: Routledge, 2001, 61.

33

Improv Rules, Major Theoretical Concepts, and Maxims

So you'll hear a lot about how there aren't really rules in improv. And that's sort of true. But there are some guiding principles that make getting on stage and spontaneously creating a world with another person a whole lot easier. Here are three basic rules (or principles) that are pretty easy to follow:

1. **Agreement:** Agree to the reality that you and your partner are creating. Improv is a lot like being a kid on a playground. If Joey says the slide is a moon lab for creating space monkeys that have rabies, all of the other kids think it's the coolest thing ever and play along. *So play along.*
2. **Make Active Rather than Passive Choices:** A lot of folks phrase this as "Don't Ask Questions." Why? Because questions require information instead of giving information. But a good question can be active and add info. So, focus less on "Don't Ask Questions" and more on "Make Active Choices." Make sure you are moving the scene along by adding new information and actively doing something. Don't just agree that the slide is a moon lab; get bitten by a rabid space monkey and see what happens. *Pull your weight.*
3. **Support Your Partner:** Follow Martin de Maat's advice and remember, "Your partner is the most important person onstage." Set each other up for success, treat his or her ideas like gold, and be ready to play along. Build one another up and take care of each other. Trust each other and earn trust. You're a team. Following rules 1 and 2 is a pretty good start.

35

Building off of these guiding principles (ahem … rules) are some major theoretical concepts about improvisation. These are some of the fundamental principles behind improvisation from a variety of schools, and understanding them will make your life on stage easier and more fruitful.

We've included a *Practice Right Now* exercise as well as a list of related exercises and games for each rule/maxim. Please note that pretty much every scene uses all of these rules and maxims. Nearly all of the exercises, games, and long form structures in the later sections will require you to use these skills, so the recommended exercises listed here are hardly the only ones you can use to sharpen your skills.

Yes, And

Often considered the main rule of improv, "Yes, And" means *play along and pull your weight.* Your partner has an idea, so you play along and add something new to the world. By saying yes, we accept the reality created by our partners and begin the collaborative process … you know, playing along. The easiest way to build a scene is to say yes to the first idea, treat it like gold, and build it together with your scene partner(s). Saying yes takes players from an invention mindset into a build and react mindset. But you can't simply say "yes" and pat yourself on the back. An improvised scene can't progress if you only say "yes"; you also must add new information. By saying "and," we are pulling our weight by actively adding new information to move the scene forward (see how "Yes, And" encapsulates the first two rules of improv? And subsequently supports your partner?). There are lots of ways to "Yes, And" during a scene that don't involve the words "Yes, and." So if all else fails remember to simply play along and pull your weight.

Practice Right Now: Get in a circle. Say a simple statement to the person on your right. That person says "yes", and adds one piece of information. Keep going around the circle adding information.

Recommended Exercises/Games: "Yes, And", "Yes, Let's", Ad Game, Three-Line Scenes, Sound Ball, Environmental Support, Machine, Freeze, Documentary – Compliment Variation.

Agreement

When an improviser begins a scene, the choices are infinite. He can play any character he chooses and so can his scene partner. At the beginning of an improvised scene, the most important thing players must accomplish is to decide on the Who, What, Where, and Why of the scene. And the most important tool for deciding those circumstances is agreement. In essence, an improviser must agree to all facts and circumstances that his or her scene partner establishes, whether through dialogue, behavior, or action. If you say we are married and that you're leaving me, then I *must* agree to those circumstances. I might get a laugh by saying "But we're not married," but that undercuts the scene and my partner's trust. Instead of agreeing and building the scene, I broke the reality for a laugh and stalled the scene. You simply cannot build a scene if the agreement is broken.

It's important to note that *agreement is between the actors, not necessarily the characters*. So that means it's okay to say "No" sometimes. If your partner says, "I need you to put me in a barrel and push me over Niagara Falls," you are agreeing with her if you say, "Barb, you've got a lot to live for. I'm not going to push you over Niagara Falls." You are still agreeing to the offer and moving the scene forward. Your partner's offer is asking you to stop her from killing herself, so by saying "No" you are actually agreeing to the offer.

Of course, you can also say, "Sure, Barb! I'm surprised it took you this long to realize your life was meaningless." Either way, you are agreeing with your partner and progressing the scene.

Practice Right Now: Stay in your circle. Now say something to the person on your left that normally would cause an argument (e.g. "I want a divorce.") Instead of fighting, agree to the offer ("Thank God! I never thought you'd ask.") Now turn to the next person and begin anew.

Recommended Exercises/Games: "Yes, And", "Yes, Let's", Ad Game, Three-Line Scenes, Sound Ball, Environmental Support, Master–Servant, One-Word Story, Conducted Story, Documentary – Compliment Variation.

Support Your Partner

One famous adage in improv is that everyone is a supporting actor. As Isaiah Thomas[1] said, "The secret about basketball is that it isn't about basketball." The best teams aren't the ones with the five most talented players – the best teams are the ones that work together harmoniously. There is a reason a bunch of guys in their mid-40s with knee braces and sports goggles can beat a more talented group of 20-year-olds at the YMCA. They work together. They support one another. They understand the nuances of the game. If Isaiah was here right now, I'm sure he'd say, "The secret of improvisation is that it isn't about being funny ... Would you like an unprotected lottery pick?"

Sorry, back to improv.

Rather than thinking only about yourself, you're always looking to support the other actors, helping them out and knowing that they too will help you. Risk taking is a lot easier when there is a team willing to jump with you. By incorporating both the rules of "Yes, And" and Agreement, the process has already begun. If your partner looks good, and he helps you look good, then together you have created a successful scene. One of the most important things to remember is that *improvisation is a team effort*. A scene or show is never successful or unsuccessful because of one person.

There are lots of ways to support your partner beyond "Yes, And" and agreement. *The best way to support your partner is to actively listen –* even when you are off stage or on the back line. If you are actively listening you will be highly responsive to what your partner needs and you won't miss anything he or she may be implicitly or explicitly asking you to provide (and she might be asking you for something you'll bring to a scene 15 minutes from now). A lot of folks follow Mick Napier's advice to take care of yourself first as the best way to support your partner. Rather than simply looking for what they need, take care of your own needs – establish who you are, where you are, and what you want. The theory goes that if you do those things, you are supporting your partner. Whatever approach you take ultimately doesn't matter; what matters is that you are working with your partner.

Practice Right Now: Let's keep the circle thing going. Turn to the person on your right and give them a gift ("I got you this puppy.") Respond as though it is the absolute perfect gift ("You found the lost puppy from my childhood!"). Keep giving more gifts and feel free to give what we would traditionally consider a crappy gift, like fingernail clippers. Let your partner support and justify your offer – but keep it honest! Don't mug or play at it – genuinely love the gift.

Recommended Exercises/Games: Hot Spot, "Yes, Let's", Machine, Ad Game, Three-Line Scenes, Give and Take, Freeze, Documentary – Compliment Variation, Mannequin.

38 Justification

There are no mistakes in improv. Everything in a scene is important so there is no such thing as a throwaway or mistake. Seasoned improvisers know that a mistake is only a mistake if it isn't used. Often a "mistake" ends up being the lynchpin of the scene. A mispronounced word, an erroneous fact, or simply tripping can become great gifts if you let them. Justification also works to support your partner by making his or her ideas valuable. Supported players tend to bring more (and better) ideas to the stage. By justifying our action and what we say (and what our partner does), players are able to progress scenes, react in the moment, and most importantly, keep the audience in on the joke.

It is important, however, to distinguish between *justification to support* and *justification to explain*. If I bring a kitten into the scene, you work with me to justify its existence. Step 1 is simply agreeing that it is there and treating it with importance. Justification to explain can kill a scene. That is when you see the kitten and immediately explain why I have the kitten. Too many beginning improvisers feel the need to explain everything. They explain the relationship, the environment/location, the plot, and/or their feelings instead of actually playing all those things. *Show – Don't Tell.* Don't explain why you are nervous around Joe – just *be nervous around Joe.* Playing the context instead of explaining it makes the scene easier to play and more enjoyable to watch – and guess what? It justifies what the players are doing. Justify by making what your partner is doing important. Use the information – don't explain it away.

For example: "Mom, I scratched the car." Justification to support would look something like this: "You scratched my baby? I'm going to kill you." Your scene partner is justifying your choice by honoring it and making the scene about the relationship between the two characters: the mom cares more about the car than her son. Justifying to explain looks like this: "Well that's okay. You were probably just trying to impress your friends and you aren't even 16 yet so you don't have your license so I can see how that might have happened." This response explains why the scratch happened instead of focusing on the relationship between the two characters. Resist the urge to explain. The scene can still work, but you are making it harder on yourself. Of course, you might recognize that explaining everything away becomes the game of the scene, which is a great choice for one particular scene, but if you are always explaining things away your scenes aren't going to work.

Practice Right Now: Break into pairs. One is the servant and one is the master. The master gives the servant orders and the servant justifies them.

> Master: "Get me some lemonade."
> Servant: "Of course; the lemons are at their
>   peak ripeness. You always know the perfect
>   time to harvest."
> Master: "That's why I'm king. Now get me my
>   fleece socks."

Recommended Exercises/Games: Entrances and Exits, Emotional Quadrants, Sit, Stand, Lie Down, Ad Game, Freeze, Trigger Word.

Status

Introduced by Keith Johnstone, status in improv refers to the power structure of a scene. There are two major types of status: high and low. One is not necessarily better than the other, but the high-status character is usually the one with the upper hand in the scene. A high-status

39

character either has what he or she wants in the scene, or has what the other person wants in the scene. Therefore, status can (and should) shift in a scene. Most scenes start with a clear status structure, feature a status swap in the middle, and end when the original high-status character either succeeds or fails in reacquiring the status. Some high-status characteristics include: stillness, control, confidence, gender, age, occupation, wealth, and friends. High-status characters tend to take up a lot of space, have good posture, keep a still head (they have less movement in general), make direct eye contact, and speak in short declarative statements. Low-status characters are fidgety, lack confidence, avoid eye contact, talk a lot (and in circles), etc. Status is dependent on the values of a society (a society that values money = wealthy people have higher status). Status is not inherent – it is given. For example, if nobody wants to sit at the "cool table" in the high school cafeteria, those kids lose their status.

Status Test!

Identify the high-status character.

1. Beth is going to ask hunky Tom to prom.
   If you answered "Tom," you are correct. Why? Because he's hunky. But also because Tom has the power to decide if Beth gets what she wants.
2. Professor Thompson has called Jody into his office to discuss her poor grade on a research paper.
   If you answered, "Professor Thompson," you're right again. He has the status due to several factors: it is *his* office; Jody has failed the paper; he is the one calling the meeting; we can assume he is older than her; he is in the power position of a traditional power structure (teacher–student); and he is the one handing out the grade.

So how can Jody take the status, and/or Professor Thompson lose the status? There are lots and lots of ways. Here are a few:

- Jody doesn't care about the grade. If the power structure relies on Jody wanting to get good grades then the power rests with the character giving out the grade. If she doesn't care about grades, he no longer has power. In fact, Jody has the power because Professor Thompson wants her to care and she doesn't.

- Jody reveals some information about Professor Thompson that he didn't know she had (she knows about an affair he's having, or that he is using Professor Barty's copy code, etc.). He now must try and put out the fire, giving her the power because she can now determine what to do with the information.
- Professor Thompson can give her an A even though she didn't earn it. If he gives away his power (i.e. his ability to grade her), then he no longer has the high status.

Practice Right Now: Two people. Use your birthday as your number (so let's say 1 is the lowest status possible and 31 is the highest). You and your partner are going to see a movie. Enter the movie theater, sit down, and try to establish your status and respond to your partner's status (remember that status is fluid). Work not only on verbalizing status, but also physicalizing it.

Recommended Exercises/Games: Status Party, Status Swap, Master–Servant.

Group Mind

Improv is a highly collaborative form. Each member of the group needs to be harmoniously working with the others and the best teams are intellectually, physically, and emotionally in synch with one another (remember the secret about basketball). Basically, group mind means that all of the players on a team are working toward the same goal by opening their awareness and creating one group mind that encapsulates each individual; it is *e pluribus unum* exemplified. Players use the intelligence of the group and the ideas of the group to create something bigger than the individual members.

Achieving a group mind requires setting aside your own ego (and critic) and giving yourself over to the team. Following others' ideas, supporting and building upon them, and doing whatever is required in performance are all part of the group mind. Players begin to anticipate what their teammates will say and do because they are connected to one another, and therefore are able to make connections in the piece that didn't seem feasible. In short, it means that the whole is greater than the sum of its parts. This is how the older guys at the YMCA keep winning their rec-league.

Practice Right Now: Get back in that circle and close your eyes. You're going to recite the alphabet, but if two people say the same letter at the same time, you have to go back to A. Resist cheating and using a basic around-the-circle pattern. Now reverse it and make it so *everyone* has to say the same letter at the same time.

Recommended Exercises/Games: Pass the Clap, Counting, Skip 3s, 1-2-3 People Walking, Run to the Middle, Caligula, Mind Meld, Patterns, A–C Patterns.

Listening and Reincorporation

Everything that happens on stage is important, and it is your job to be aware of everything because a good improviser knows that whatever happens on stage can and will be used again. And this is why virtually every improv teacher in the world stresses the importance of listening. Truly listening to your partner and responding in the moment is the best way to build a scene, remain grounded in honesty, have an emotional response, and achieve a successful scene.

Listening is more than just listening to words – you must listen not only to what is said, but *how* it is said. Listen to your partner's body language, energy, and movements. If you aren't listening in all of these ways, you are making improv harder than it needs to be and chances are your scenes will be unsuccessful. Often a beginning improviser will step on stage with a fully formed idea and pursue it regardless of what his or her scene partner does. That's bulldozing a scene. Instead of listening and reacting in the moment, you are writing a sketch and forcing the other person to be in it with you. That's not a really fun way to play and it is painfully awkward to watch. If you have a great sketch idea, go write a sketch – don't force it on your scene partner.

Taking an idea, phrase, or something else and repeating it throughout the piece, known as a callback or reincorporation,[2] is at the heart of performing improvisation, especially long form improvisation. Improv is about making connections, so listening to what is happening and then using (and reusing) that information becomes the backbone of the art form.

Practice Right Now: Pick another buddy. One of you takes about 30 seconds and begins telling a story. After 30 seconds the partner picks up the story and using the elements introduced, continues the story. Keep switching back and forth every 30 seconds. The story ends when you've reincorporated all of the elements of the story. Now tell a new story to your partner without words.

Recommended Exercises/Games: A–B, Ad Game, Color/Advance, Repetition, Give and Take, Back-to-Back Chairs, Last Letter–First Letter, Alphabet Game, That's Important to Me.

Truth in Comedy

Nothing is less funny than someone trying to be funny. Think of your uncomfortable uncle at Thanksgiving who thinks puns are the highest form of comedy. You're trying not to tell your grandmother that you're an Art/Theater double major with a minor in Midwest Studies and he bursts out "Slow down soldier! If you put too much on your turkey, you will be in 'gravy' danger." Hilarious, right? Now think of the times that you have laughed the hardest. Was it at a joke or pun? Probably not. It was probably in a real-life situation (or recalling said situation).

iO espouses that "The truth is funny," arguing that "we're funniest when we're just being ourselves. Sitting around relaxing with friends usually inspires far more laughter than a TV sitcom or someone trying to tell jokes."[3] People respond to honesty, truth, and vulnerability. They are your greatest comedic weapons on stage. Even Mr. Rodgers agrees: "One of the greatest gifts you can give anybody is the gift of your honest self." Mr. Rodgers is always right, you guys.

Practice Right Now: Tell your teammates an embarrassing personal story. Don't make it up.

Recommended Exercises/Games: I Remember, Back-to-Back Chairs, Monologues, That's Important to Me, Heat and Weight.

43

The Game of the Scene

The game of the scene, which is akin to a comedic premise, simply means that the players are agreeing to the comic element of the scene, or what makes the scene funny. There are some differences concerning the game of the scene between Chicago and New York, however, so let's look at the two schools of thought. In Chicago, the game is generally associated with anything that repeats in a scene, and can be a scenic or character element. A scene can exist without a game.

In New York, led by UCB, the game *is* the scene. The game is generally the first unusual thing in a scene, and becomes "the funny" in the scene. The UCB focuses on three questions to find and play the game: What is the basic situation or "base reality?" What is the first unusual thing about the scene? If that is true, then what else is true? For example, "If a football player is afraid of contact, what else might he be afraid of that is implicitly part of his job?" The game then becomes, "Being afraid of what is necessary for your job."

Ideally each scene will have a base reality, something that is familiar to everyone such as a typical father–son conversation, or doctor–patient exchange, etc. It is then up to the players to initially play out the scene according to those rules, but to stay alert so that they can recognize the first unusual thing that happens in the scene. For instance, the son seems to be giving his father advice, or the doctor is revealing personal information to the patient. Once the game has been established – and often the players call out the game, "I didn't think you were going to share that about your wife, Doctor" – the players then push the game by looking for variations and ways to heighten or raise the stakes. The doctor might give more and more intimate details about his personal life, for instance, that mirror and heighten those of the patient. While it sounds simple, recognizing and playing the game of the scene is a difficult skill. Before you make it too complex, remember that often the game is rather simple, so follow the advice of the folks over at PeopleandChairs.com, "Find something fun, then do it more."

Practice Right Now: Do your best to recreate Abbott & Costello's *Who's on First?* Don't worry about getting the bit "right"; instead focus on how the game of confusing names is played. Now take the game of confusing names and put it in new situations (maybe you are giving directions and all the street names are directions themselves).

Recommended Exercises/Games: Nearly any short form game works here as the structure includes "the game" – simply identify what element is "the game." For instance, in a guessing game, "the game" is the fact that one or more players don't know particular information. In Emotional Quadrants "the game" is the fact that one character keeps shifting emotions depending on where she is on the stage (of course there can be scenic games within short form, but the structure itself provides players a game to play). Practice identifying what the players are using to make the scene humorous – that's the game. Then transfer that skill to long form structures where "the game" isn't inherently built into the structure.

Play to the Top of Your Intelligence

A famous Del Close adage, this does not mean that every character you play has to be as brilliant and witty as you. It does mean that you need to make the character as intelligent as he or she can possibly be (because you are brilliant and witty). Don't make fun of your character – understand your character. When players go on stage they tend to have a bit of fear or anxiety about messing up or not being funny, and this causes them to go to wacky town and make obvious, insincere, or broad choices. They play the generic stupid southern farmer who is racist, and then as a performer simply make fun of the character. That's playing to the lowest common denominator.

Try making the unexpected choice instead of the obvious choice. Play a cracker-jack southern farmer championing civil rights. It's simply more interesting. Playing to the top of your intelligence means making choices that come from honesty and truth, that reflect real life and the inner life of your character. For example, we've all seen the scene where a player has to sing or dance on the spot. Usually the player cops out and purposefully does it badly because he thinks that will be funny. Usually it is just awkward for everyone. Instead, sing or dance to the best of your ability. Make it truthful and honest. The audience will respond because they will see your commitment, vulnerability, and honesty.

This also means that you need to play to the top of your audience's intelligence. Don't underestimate them. They are smarter than you think they are. They will get references you think they won't. Don't worry if every person in the audience doesn't get your John Jay reference; somebody will and it'll make their day. *Play up instead of playing down.*

Practice Right Now: Improvise a character monologue that plays against stereotypes. In fact, give a monologue that goes against one of your personal beliefs and do your best to imbue it with honesty and integrity.

Recommended Exercises/Games: I Remember, Back-to-Back Chairs, Silent Connection, Three-Line Scenes, Heat and Weight.

Originality

There are three basic theories about originality in improvisation: Del Close's "Slow Comedy," Keith Johnstone's "Spontaneity," and Mick Napier's "Do Something!"

Close wanted to break the joke-based system of comedy found in stand-up. He sought to do this by developing a system of comedy based on intellectual connections. In other words, he wanted to slow things down. Close's concept is that your first thought is a knee-jerk reaction, and probably based on a joke. The second thought is a bit better, but still not right. The third thought is the best thought because you've had time to process the situation. As noted in *Truth in Comedy*, "if a player takes the time to consider what the other speaker means, then his response is more intelligent … a more carefully considered response takes a second or two longer, but the wait is well worth it."[4]

Theatresports founder Keith Johnstone argues in *Impro* that improvisers should say the first thing that comes into their heads. Johnstone thinks that originality stems from individuals' own experiences, and improvisers that search for the "right" response or a clever response end up in trouble, and often come up with less original or humorous ideas. Originality, for Johnstone, is often about voicing our own unique perspectives while at the same time meeting the audience's expectations.[5]

The third theory comes from The Annoyance co-founder Mick Napier, author of *Improvise*, who argues that what improvisers do is not nearly as important as that they simply "Do something!" Overthinking leads to fear, clichés, and timid performance. Reacting honestly in the moment with "something" is the best way to keep a scene moving and the audience engaged. Simply doing something will "snap you out of your head."[6]

While many have pitted Close, Johnstone, and Napier against one another, they actually are after the same idea: an honest reaction.[7] Close's whole idea was that for a trained improviser the first thought that pops into their head should actually be their third thought. Slow comedy didn't mean that the show had to be slow. It simply meant that performers had to carefully consider their responses. If a performer could do slow fast, if he or she could process those three thoughts quickly, then he or she could go as fast as his or her mind allowed. In the end, each of them wanted improvisers who were honest and who reacted to his or her partner truthfully. They had slightly different ideas about how to do that, but were after the same goal.

So those are the basic theories and tenets of improvisation. There are more, but if you don't master these the other ones don't matter. But wait, there's more! There are also a bunch of improv maxims that can be especially helpful for new improvisers. Most of them try to boil down these theories and rules into a simple phrase that can often be a little more manageable.

Some Simple Maxims

Sometimes it's easy to get stuck in your head. Trying to follow the rules/guidelines/theories/etc. can be overwhelming. Of course, with practice the rules become second nature. And that's kind of the point. Any of these rules can be broken in a scene. A good improviser doesn't consciously think "I'm going to break rule X here to get a laugh." Nobody would suggest playing football – either American or soccer – without rules. A quarterback, from Tim Tebow to Tom Brady, doesn't think about how to throw a football when he drops back to pass. He doesn't think about any of the rules of the game or the mechanics of throwing a football. He relies on muscle memory and instincts. A good improviser does the same. So maxim 1 is …

Rehearse

Yup, improvisers need to rehearse. Your friends, family, and coworkers will continually misunderstand what it is you are doing – and the biggest misconception is about rehearsal. "Isn't it all made up? So what do you rehearse?" You'll answer this question about three million times in your lifetime. You rehearse to get better. You rehearse to instinctively learn the rules of improv. You rehearse to create muscle memory. You rehearse to create group mind. You rehearse to learn new structures or create new forms. You rehearse for the same reason musicians rehearse, athletes practice, and children lie – to get better at your craft. At minimum you should be rehearsing with your group once a week for two hours. The more time you spend together, both in and outside of rehearsal, the better. Remember, the secret about basketball …

Have an Emotional Point of View

You need to have a strong emotional point of view in a scene. You feel a certain way about the other person in the scene and/or the situation of the scene. That feeling can morph and change as the scene progresses, but if you start at neutral you're making the scene harder than it needs to be. Giving yourself a strong emotional point of view gives you something to play in the scene without having to invent.

You can discover that emotion at the top of the scene and let it build, or you can enter the scene with an emotional point of view (so long as you aren't manipulating the scene or trying to force a particular idea/storyline, it isn't cheating and it'll work). Your emotional intensity can vary on a 1–10 scale, so don't feel like you have to be ANGRY or IN LOVE like an insane person right from the top, and of course different people express emotions in different ways. Having an emotional point of view:

1. Starts the action of the scene faster. If I enter and have a strong emotion, the scene is already in progress, as opposed to entering neutral and waiting for something to happen
2. Gives your partner something to play against and react to. You have two options in terms of emotion – match your partner or play opposite – and then of course to push their emotion further. If your partner is mad, you make them madder
3. Raises the stakes of the scene. If you actually care, there is more for you to lose, which inevitably raises the stakes and makes the scene more interesting
4. Puts the audience at ease because they can see something is in the works. If nothing is happening on stage, the audience gets nervous. If you have an emotion, something is happening, so the audience thinks you know what you are doing.

48

Sample Emotions: Adoring, Alarmed, Alienated, Amorous, Amused, Astonished, Attached, Bitter, Bossy, Compassionate, Confident, Courageous, Defeated, Devastated, Disdainful, Disillusioned, Dismayed, Distressed, Doting, Eager, Elated, Enthralled, Envious, Exhilarated, Fatigued, Frightened, Frustrated, Furious, Gleeful, Gloomy, Grumpy, Guilty, Hesitant, Hopeful, Hostile, Humiliated, Hysterical, Idolizing, Inadequate, Inquisitive, Insecure, Irritated, Judgmental, Motivated, Nervous, Nostalgic, Outraged, Overwhelmed, Passionate, Pensive, Perplexed, Rejected, Relieved, Remorseful, Resentful, Revolted, Shocked, Skeptical, Spiteful, Stupefied, Suspicious, Tender, Terrified, Thrilled, Triumphant, Violated, Vulnerable, Withdrawn, and Worried.

Practice Right Now: Get in a circle and only call each other by name. Use a strong emotional point of view when you say the name. See how much information is there (and see how strong of a reaction you have when another member says your name with feeling).

Recommended Exercises/Games: Initiations, Three-Line Scenes, Enemy–Protector, Heightening Game, That's Important to Me, Emotional Build, Oscar Moment, Emotional Quadrants, Heat and Weight.

React!

The best way to make a scene work, to highlight a particular moment, or to simply progress the scene is to react to what your partner is saying. A boring stalled scene suddenly becomes interesting when a player reacts. Your reaction can be as big or small as you'd like – more important is that it is an honest reaction. As Del Close said, "Honest discovery, observation, and reaction is better than contrived invention." A drop of honesty goes a long way. You can react to anything, however seemingly big, small, or trivial.

Reacting gives weight to what is happening and instantly heightens the relationship in the scene. That means you have to be fully listening in a scene – and not just to the words. Remember, *what* is said in a scene is not nearly as important as *how* it is said. "It's supposed to rain today" can mean a million different things depending on how you say it. So stop reacting blindly to information and start reacting to the energy and intention – react to the *how* (this is what TJ & Dave refer to as the "weight" of a scene).

Most everyday relationships unfold in this way – we react to the energy we are being given, not necessarily the information. If your boyfriend is in a bad mood, you react to that mood, not to the literal things he's saying. We've all been there before when we ask someone what's wrong and he or she says "Nothing." Are you completely convinced when he says "nothing"? Or do you listen and respond to the energy he is giving you? You respond to the how. Think about it: more often than not a single line isn't funny. It is the reaction to the line that is funny or interesting (and the reaction to the reaction and so on). And that reaction is easier, funnier, and more honest if it is coming from the energy in the scene. Don't believe us? Think about all of the films you've watched and how they are edited. Do we stay with the person speaking, or more often than not, do we cut to the listener to see his or her reaction to what is being said? Reactions work on film and they work on stage. Reacting makes your scene work stronger and funnier – and the dirty little secret? Reacting makes the scene easier to play for the improvisers.

But it only really works if you are reacting honestly. Channel your inner-Stanislavski and ask yourself, "If I was in this situation, how would I react?" We don't need your reactions to take us to wacky town. In real life, if your best friend told you he was getting kicked out of school, how would you honestly react? For some reason in

49

improv we like to take those reactions to extremes – we take the scene to wacky town. Instead, stay true to your character and react honestly. Don't be afraid to let a line land, or to take a moment to process – that's what people do in actual everyday life. How many times do TJ & Dave take a scene to wacky town?

Practice Right Now: Start a scene with relatively bland lines. Within the first four, one of the characters should react to a seemingly meaningless line. See how the scene takes off.

```
1: Pretty cloudy today, George.
2: Yeah, a bit chilly too.
1: Guess we're stuck inside.
2: (Pauses. Something is clearly wrong.)
1: What?
2: I can't be in that house anymore, Bill. You
   know that.
```

And the scene begins. Simply by reacting to being "stuck inside" leads to a discovery, and that discovery leads to the meat of the scene.

Practice Right Now – Part II: Player 1 starts an action. Player 2 enters and says "We're out of milk." Player 1 – let the line land and let your reaction be honest. Listen to *the way* Player 2 said the line. Was it deathly serious? Was he annoyed? Was it playful? Again, *how* the line is said is more important than the actual dialogue. Player 2, it is helpful if you think of a scenario that is leading you into the scene – did you two have a big fight last night, or get engaged, etc.?

Recommended Exercises/Games: Initiations, Three-Line Scenes, Enemy–Protector, Heightening Game, That's Important to Me, Emotional Build, Oscar Moment, Emotional Quadrants, Heat and Weight.

Take it Personally

As long as you are reacting, take it personally. Listen like you are on a first date. Listen like you are a therapist. Listen like you are standing outside of your daughter's room while she is in there with that boy Tyler you don't like with the calloused hands supposedly "studying." Everything the other person is saying is laced with meaning, and everything she is saying should be personal for your character.

A personal reaction is far more interesting than a broad generic reaction (or neutral indifference) because it will be more specific and more honest. Again, a drop of honesty goes miles farther than a giant insincere reaction. Make sure to name one another in the scene – the earlier the better. Once you name someone, you instantly build a history. It's difficult to have an emotional personal reaction to a stranger. It's easy to have a personal emotional reaction to creepy Mike from accounting who's always hanging around the vending machine eating Funyuns (just giving him a name suddenly fills in a lot of other details). Say their name with feeling. Endow it with emotion. See how much you can discover about your scene partner by just bitterly saying, "Michelle." Or saying it with unbridled glee.

Practice Right Now: Go ahead. Make two lines, enter a scene, and only say one another's name with some sort of emotion (hint: you don't always have to be pissed at the other person). Don't say anything else for ten seconds and do your best to keep eye contact. Notice all of the stuff that is there for you two to play without having to invent anything. The emotion, the relationship, and the personal connection are all there for you. Then go ahead and improvise the rest of the scene using those first ten seconds as the foundation for your scene.

Recommended Exercises/Games: Back-to-Back Chairs, Initiations, Three-Line Scenes, Enemy–Protector, Heightening Game, That's Important to Me, Emotional Build, Oscar Moment, Emotional Quadrants, Heat and Weight.

51

React, Don't Act

Just one more maxim to reinforce how important it is to react in improv scenes. Listen to what your partner is saying, and react to it like it matters. Stop being the neutral detached guy in scenes and react. Whenever Mike eats a Funyun, it should disgust you. He keeps eating them and you keep getting more and more disgusted. Or maybe it turns you on. And every Funyun that crosses his lips is ecstasy. He wipes the Funyon crumbs on his pants and you can hardly keep your clothes on. Either way, react to it and build. Instead of looking for something new to invent, simply react to what is already there. Look at all the great things you've got to play with in this scene simply by reacting to Mike eating Funyuns … and don't pretend like you don't want to see the Funyun foreplay scene.

Practice Right Now: One person stands in the middle of the circle. Everyone else peppers this person with lines and creates a scene with him or her (so the person in the middle is simultaneously in six, seven, eight scenes at once). Don't go easy on them. Don't wait for your turn. Pummel him or her and make him react as quickly as possible. They won't have time to do anything but react.

Recommended Exercises/Games: Initiations, Three-Line Scenes, Enemy–Protector, Heightening Game, That's Important to Me, Emotional Build, Oscar Moment, Emotional Quadrants, Heat and Weight.

Why You Two? Why Now?

If you are in a scene and you cannot answer why it needs to happen between these two characters, and why it needs to be happening right now, then your scene is probably boring your audience. The scene is happening between *these two characters* at *this exact moment* for a reason. Discover it and the scene will fly. Remember that your relationship is personal and unique. Don't get caught in the title of the relationship. There are a million different mother–son relationships – your relationship is how you interact and feel about one another (this is what TJ & Dave refer to as the "heat" of a relationship). It is about your history, your present, and your future. It is not about the title. We are only seeing two minutes of this very specific and unique relationship – so make it count. Hint! A good way to justify "Why you two? Why now?" is to react to what is happening in the scene on a personal level (like being turned on by Mike's Funyuns). Every scene in a play or movie is happening between two specific people at a specific moment in time – your improv scenes should too.

Practice Right Now: Do a two-person scene. Now take the time to talk about what the scene is actually about – answer "Why you two? Why now?" The more you practice it, the quicker you will find it in scenes. Go see shows and identify it for each scene. Compare notes. Feel adventurous? Try stopping the scene whenever you and your partner feel like you can answer the question – name it – and then go back to the scene. See how early you and your partner can identify what your scene is about.

Recommended Exercises/Games: Back-to-Back Chairs, Three-Line Scenes, Four Square, That's Important to Me, Heat and Weight.

Do Something. Do it More. Do it Bigger.

Matt Holmes gave us this maxim at a workshop and it simply means at the top of a scene you kind of need to do something. Once you establish that something, your best bet is to do it more. And the best way to end your scene is to do it bigger. So if you are clumsy tripping guy, keep being the clumsy tripping guy. Everything that happens in some way relates to or causes you to trip. The further (and often more absurd) this goes, the more the audience enjoys it. Do it bigger simply means find a way to up the intensity, or find an unexpected way to keep pushing. Maybe you fall down an entire building's flight of stairs, or you cause the president to trip, or any other much better example that you can think of. Audiences appreciate when you call-back or reincorporate something. They laugh when you do it in an unexpected way.

Recommended Exercises/Games: Four Square, Half-Life, Entrances and Exits, Emotional Quadrants, The Weinberg.

Make it Worse

Beginning improvisers like to invent a crisis or problem in a scene, and then to immediately solve it. You know what? Those scenes are boring. If your character is in trouble, instead of trying to solve the problem, make it worse. *Comedy is built on making situations worse.* As Kristen Schier told us during a workshop, "Celebrate human stupidity. We do so many wonderfully stupid things – that's what makes us human." That doesn't mean play stupid or dumb things down – it means celebrate humanity's flaws.

Pop Quiz! If I am a slob and it makes your character angry, should I:

A) Solve the problem by cleaning up and making nice; or
B) Make a bigger mess?

If you answered B, you are correct. The character might think he is solving the problem, but the actor should know that the "solution" is actually going to make it worse (this is one example of what we mean by play to the top of your intelligence). My character might try to clean up the mess, but I use a filthy rag to wipe the table – "Did I just use that on the floor? You bet I did. Two birds with one stone!" I sneeze on the dishes as I'm putting them away. I trip and spill the contents of the dustpan all over you. Everything I do is making the situation worse, and making your character angrier. The messier I am, the angrier you get (do something, do it more, do it bigger) and the more fun the scene is to play and watch. Audiences love seeing things get comedically worse. Think of every comedy you've ever

53

seen. Do things generally get better for the protagonist, or do they get worse? Stop solving problems and start making them worse.

Practice Right Now: Buddy up and make the first line of the scene a problem (even though we generally don't love problem scenes): "My car is full of sand!" Now within the next five lines do your absolute best to exacerbate the situation and push it as far as you can – don't solve the problem!

Recommended Exercises/Games: Master–Servant, Four Square, Evil Twin, Ding.

Commit to Your Shit

As Susan Messing says, "comedy comes from commitment and recommitment to your shit." To make an improv scene work, players need to invest in the scene 100 percent. You are creating something from nothing, and if we can see that you don't believe in it or you don't care about it, then we won't either. Beginning improvisers tend to hold back their commitment just in case the scene doesn't work, which of course makes the scene not work. Singing and dancing is a great example. If a player is required to sing or dance in a scene, he tends to default into purposefully singing/dancing badly because he thinks it's funny. What he's really doing is not committing to the scene. It doesn't matter if you can sing/dance or not; sing/dance to the best of your ability. It will be honest and vulnerable, and make your scene work because you are committed to your character.

If you are angry in the scene, then own it and be angry. Don't be detached angry – be ANGRY (and of course recognize that there are different ways to express ANGRY)! Don't make cheap jokes about it, apologize for it (as the actor … see bad singing), comment on it (as the actor), or skate around it – own it. *Commit to your action, to your partner, to the reality of the scene, and to your reactions*. If you are 100 percent invested in the scene, the odds of it working go up exponentially. Speak loudly, clearly, and with confidence. Don't step out of the scene and "comment" on it. We don't need your personal asides that show us how witty and cool (and detached) you are – we need you fully invested in what is happening. If your character wants a macadamia nut, then you better pursue that with all of your energy, intelligence, and truth … you know, play to the top of your intelligence. Often the comedy in the scene comes from the character's investment in a seemingly small thing – Darlene's desperation for a macadamia nut is funny.

Practice Right Now: Sing a song for your team. Don't do it in character. Don't try to be funny. Sing it to the best of your ability, whatever that may be.

Recommended Exercises/Games: I Remember, That's Important to Me, Any Guessing Game, Realtor, Baby Ariel, Dual Situations.

Stop Inventing and Play What's There

Sometimes we make improv harder than it needs to be. Remember that Del Close quote? You know, this one: "Honest discovery, observation, and reaction is better than contrived invention." Instead of relying on invention, start playing what is already there – see the Funyun foreplay scene, for example. Something amazing is happening between you and your partner. Discover it instead of inventing it.

TJ & Dave often talk about how they simply step into the world that already exists on stage. Own the choice you make at the top of the scene and reinvest in it throughout. Enter a scene, see what is on your partner's face, and play it. If your partner enters the scene and they look a little nervous, then your job in the scene is to push his or her nervousness (make it worse). Then simply take turns responding and reacting to one another. *Don't try to invent something new; play what is already there.*

Similarly, if you or your partner gives a gift at the top of the scene – play it. For instance, "Barry, I think we need to have a talk about your behavior." You have been given a gift. You no longer have to invent, you are Barry who disappoints people through his behavior. Maybe it is inappropriate. Maybe it is totally appropriate and that's the issue. You can discover that in the scene. For now, you simply need to play someone who needs to be talked to about his behavior. If you start a scene and you are really happy, stick to it. Even if your partner says "I'm so sorry that I blew up your house," remember that you are happy. That happiness is already there, so play it. "Sorry? I was three months behind on my mortgage." Be sure to make it honest and it'll work. If the honest move for you in the moment is to let the news crush you, then let it crush you. But don't forget or pretend like you weren't happy initially. Let it be all the more crushing because two seconds ago the world was your oyster.

That goes for object work as well as emotional point of view. If you are starting a fire, or taking a shower, or entering numbers on your computer – don't drop it. Beginning improvisers are famous for dropping whatever they are doing at the top of a scene the moment their

55

scene partner starts doing something. They cross over to their scene partner and stand next to her. This happens in part because beginning improvisers are trying to be great scene partners and want to support the shit out of whatever is happening (even though dropping what you brought for no reason is one of the worst ways to support), or they are really insecure, or they instantly assume that whatever their scene partner says is better than whatever they have to say.

Instead, own your choice and invest in it. Reinvest in yourself. Keith Johnstone argues that instead of looking forward when you are lost or confused, you should look backward. If you start the scene a little afraid, reinvest in it. Whenever you feel lost or like the scene is going off course, reinvest in whatever you did at the top. Keep doing it. For instance, you start a scene by changing a tire. You're trying to loosen a lug nut and your partner enters and starts brushing his teeth. Don't drop changing the tire and for the love of God don't explain it away! First of all, everyone saw you changing a tire so don't pretend like it didn't happen. Second, if you drop it you now have to invent something new instead of playing what is already there. Third, if you explain it away we lose the discovery that's waiting to happen and you break the reality of the scene. Instead – reinvest! You gave the scene a gift – play that gift instead of trying to find a new one.

As Rob Norman of Second City Toronto argues, one of the best ways you can support your partner is by playing consistently – and that means reinvesting and committing to what you brought to the top of the scene. Don't invent, don't explain, and don't drop what you are doing and change mid-scene – invest and reinvest and discover. *Believe in yourself.* Keep changing the tire (and keep whatever emotional point of view you had). Take your time doing it. Don't rush. Remember the *how* is important.[8] Instead of dropping and adopting what your partner is doing (or simply standing next to her), make your action be happening *because* of your scene partner, not in spite of her. There is a beautiful discovery waiting to happen in this tire changing/teeth brushing scene. I want to see what's going to happen between these two people. The audience wants to see what's going to happen between these two people. So let us see it play out.

Practice Right Now: Two players take the stage with their backs to one another. They each start doing an independent action. They then slowly turn to see what the other is doing (they of course keep performing their own action). They then begin a scene without dropping their action. The goal is to use the actions so that we know "Why

56

you two? Why now?" Don't feel the need to immediately explain it away. Use it. Let the scene play out – make your action be happening *because* of your partner.

Double Practice: Walk around campus. Look at people and identify what's going on with them (so less, "That guy is sitting under a tree" and more "That guy looks like he just passed a test he thought he'd fail." "She looks like she doesn't want to talk to anybody." "That professor is desperate for students to recognize him.") Start reading people and the energy they are giving off.

Listen (to the words, to the action/physicality, and to the energy) and you'll see all of the small cues that are present in every scene that we too often skip over in favor of invention. Keep it simple and just play what's there.

Recommended Exercises/Games: Three-Line Scenes, Counter Circles, I Remember, That's Important to Me, Silent Connection, Heat and Weight.

Keep it Simple

There is a lot to do in an improv scene, and it is tempting to play a scene with a checklist in your head. This is part of the reason Mick Napier and other folks dislike rules. Am I saying yes? Am I adding new info? Am I following all the maxims you just told me about? In the end, you need to keep it simple: own what you bring, react to what is there, and have fun. You are better off starting a scene with "You don't look so good, Barb" than some overly complicated initiation that gives your partner too much information, such as "Albert, my best friend since fourth grade and current co-worker, I just downloaded a virus to all of the company computers. Everyone is going to crash and the company is going to lose everything. We need to go fix it or you won't get that big promotion you need to pay off your gambling debts!"

This might seem like a good offer because it establishes who you are and what's going on, but it's not. It not only gives your partner too many things to respond to, it also plans out the scene. Now everybody knows exactly what's going to happen … and the audience is going to be bored. And you are probably going to be bored. "You don't look so good, Barb" gives plenty of info to start a scene and more importantly allows room for discovery. It allows you to be surprised by what your scene partner will do. Discovery + Surprise = Fun. And that's why we do improv. And that's why people watch improv. Don't forget to have fun! Keep it simple and play what's there!

Practice Right Now: Best or Worst – A variant of Rob Norman's Love/Hate: Your scene partner starts the scene: "The sink is full of dishes, honey." Your response is simple: is this the best thing in the world or the worst? Remember, everything is about the relationship that is happening between you two *right now*. This scene isn't about dirty dishes: it's about the relationship between this couple. So you can respond with a Best: "Sweetie, I want to hang on to the magic of last night a little longer." Or with a Worst: "I'm not your slave, I'm your husband." Either way, the scene is about the relationship, not the object. Try it.

Recommended Exercises/Games: Initiations, Three-Line Scenes, Back-to-Back Chairs.

Risk Failure

It happens to all of us – we get stuck in improv ruts. Or we get afraid in front of an audience and default to what has worked in the past. We play the same characters in the same type of scene over and over. Beginning improvisers tend to cling to their first successful type and play it again and again. So try risking failure. Risk playing serious. Risk not going for laughs. Risk silence. Risk dropping something heavy on your scene partner (and the audience). Risk dropping something really weird. Risk playing out of your comfort zone. Risk really meticulous object work. Risk celebrating the mundane. Risk actually reacting honestly. Risk allowing yourself to make a mistake. Risk not being perfect.

And finally …

Remember You Are You

Don't forget that *you* are in the scene. Everything you know, you feel, you've experienced (and are experiencing) is available for you to use in a scene. If you are having a great day, don't try to mask it on stage. If you are having a shitty day, instead of trying to hide it or pretend it isn't there, use it – break down in the scene and shovel fistfuls of Funyuns in your mouth. People respond to truth, so play your truth instead of trying to hide it.[9]

Because you are you, continue to build and better your non-improv self. You spend about 99 percent of your life off stage, so live it. You can't play to the top of your intelligence if you don't know anything. Take advantage of your non-theater/improv classes. Look at them as opportunities to enlarge your improv brain. You never know when knowing about the Peloponnesian War will come in handy in a scene, or knowing how light is refracted will be the lynchpin of your scenic relationship, or when knowing the life cycle of potatoes will be the funniest thing you ever do on stage.

Read a lot of books. Read novels, poetry, non-fiction. Read something you wouldn't normally read. Follow the news. Know what is happening in the world, in the country, in your city, and on your campus.

Observe. Observe people. Watch how they behave.

Go out and explore. Go to a new restaurant. Go to a museum. Go to a neighborhood you've never been to and walk around (but don't be stupid about it). Seek out events. Go to the Prime Beef Parade, or whatever community-specific celebrations your town holds. Go to the farmer's market. Go to Home Depot. Go to specialty stores. There are entire worlds and sub-cultures out there waiting for you to find out about them.

Talk to new people. Interview your professors – they tend to be fascinating people (and usually love talking about themselves). Pay attention to your family – even the crazy ones. Your libertarian uncle who thinks 9/11 was an inside job is a character study waiting to happen. Don't mock him – understand where his views are coming from. Seek out people who view the world differently than you. Make friends with a Republican. Make non-improv friends. Cultivate non-improv interests. Have hobbies. If all you have to bring to the stage is improv, then you're not bringing anything to the stage. The best improvisers in the world are intellectually curious people. There are only so many meta-scenes you can do – so go out and live!

59

Some Common Don't Scenes

While the maxims give you something to work toward in scenes, there are also some things you should try to avoid in scenes. Here are a few "don't" scene types that you'll hear along your journey. These types of scenes tend not to work. That doesn't mean you can't ever do one – they are just a lot harder and have a much lower rate of success.

Transaction Scenes

If all that happens in your scene is one character buying something from another, you have a pretty boring scene on your hands. The reason these scenes fail is because the players tend to focus on the transaction instead of the relationship between the two characters. It can be difficult to establish a relationship because most transactions don't last that long and occur between strangers. If you find yourself in a transaction scene that is all about the pack of gum you are buying, have a personal emotional reaction to the next line. Start your line with "I, You or We." Maybe you are buying the gum because you are trying to stall before your wedding and you heard that a clerk at this store gave great wedding advice – at least then you can confide in the clerk. Or discover that you know the clerk, are attracted to the clerk, or despise the clerk. You can also use the fact that you have a want in the scene (a pack of gum) and heighten it so that you *need* the pack of gum. Whatever you do, make the scene about the two people on stage, not about what one character happens to be buying.

Practice Right Now: 2 players – one is a store clerk and the other a customer returning an item. Make the scene about the two people in the scene, not the item being returned. Use the item to push the relationship.

> A: "Candace, funny seeing you here."
> B: "Well, I've got to support myself now."
> A: "Yeah … This spatula isn't working for me."
> B: "Too loyal?"
> A: "No, it's got no give. It's too rigid."

And so on – this scene is about the breakup that these two clearly aren't over yet, not about returning a spatula.

Teaching Scenes

Audiences are not interested in watching you teach your scene partner how to make a sandwich. These scenes are a lot easier to fall into than transaction scenes. The second one character says he doesn't know how to do something, the immediate reaction is to teach him how to do it. You think to yourself, "Just imagine how funny it'll be when I show him how to make a sandwich and he still can't do it!" Meanwhile the audience is bored watching you teach someone how to make a sandwich. There is no personal connection between the characters, which instantly makes the scene boring. Think about all the scenes in movies where a guy is "teaching" a gal how to shoot pool/swing a bat or golf club/play beach volleyball. What is he really doing? He's trying to seduce the woman, not teach her a particular skill. Teaching scenes can work if the scene is about something besides teaching the task at hand. If a wife is trying to tell her husband she wants a divorce by teaching him how to do the dishes, the scene can work because it's not about teaching.

Practice Right Now: Do the same practice as above, but instead of a transaction, one partner is teaching the other how to bake a cake, change a tire, fold a sweater (or something) – but remember the scene is about the relationship, not teaching the activity.

61

It's My First ...

Most firsts don't work on stage because they lead to teaching scenes. "It's my first day on the job" leads the other character to feel like they have to show you the ropes. Most firsts don't work because the characters have no history, they fall into neutral states, and they lead to teaching scenes. We also like to start scenes in the middle of something, not at the very beginning of something. Teaching scenes tend to start at the beginning. And the beginning of scenes is usually boring because nothing is happening yet between the characters.

Practice Right Now: Stop saying it's your first day. Or start a scene saying it is your first day and the next line immediately establishes a personal connection between the characters that is far more important than teaching the newbie the ropes. Maybe you are starting at your dad's company, your ex is your boss, or your supervisor is the sexiest person alive.

The Quest or Problem Scene

Going on an epic journey isn't the best thing to watch on an improv stage ... mainly because players end up talking a lot about the quest instead of actually doing anything about it. Same goes for the problem scene. "Oh no, we have to defuse this bomb!" The danger with the problem scene is that the scene then becomes completely about defusing the bomb. Make sure that you still make a personal connection with your scene partner and that there is something happening between the characters ... who also just so happen to be defusing a bomb. I'd much rather watch a scene between two brothers who feel like their father loved the other one best trying to "win" at defusing a bomb than two generic characters trying to defuse a bomb.

Practice Right Now: There is a bank robbery in progress. Do a scene that isn't about the bank robbery, but is about the relationship – something about the bank robbery forces the scene to be about the relationship (much like defusing the bomb forces the sibling rivalry to come to the surface).

Doing an Activity ... And Talking About It

You should be physically doing something in a scene. Always. Let me repeat that. You should be physically doing something in a scene. But that doesn't mean I want to hear you talk about it. Because it's boring. And you'll probably try to teach. So by all means, bake that cake, fix that carburetor – just don't talk about it. You can be re-tiling your bathroom – just don't make the scene about re-tiling your bathroom. Your son might be helping you. Let the scene be about your relationship – however unhealthy or healthy it may be. Use the activity to heighten the relationship, not as a crutch to fall back on.

Practice Right Now: Two characters are pitching a tent. They aren't allowed to talk about pitching the tent.

The Talking Heads

Remember when we just said that you should always physically be doing something in a scene? Well, if you don't, you fall prey to the talking heads scene. Good band. Boring scenes. Like all of these examples, you can have a successful talking heads scene. But you are making things a lot harder on yourself because if you aren't physically doing anything, then everything that happens in the scene must come verbally. That is a lot of pressure. There is a reason most great comedians all have physical bits. If you ever hit a speed bump in a talking heads scene, you don't have anything to do. You just end up standing there – and then the audience can tell that you don't have anything, and then they lose confidence in you and start to worry... and when they are worried about you, they aren't engaged or laughing.

Practice Right Now: Spolin time! Contact! Do a scene. Before every line, somebody must do some sort of physical action.

Wacky Town, USA

Beginning improvisers like to make things wacky and zany right away in a scene. They forgo honesty and go straight for the crazy. Every reaction is over-the-top-out-of-control-in-no-way-shape-or-form-honest-or-real. "Relationship? Who needs a relationship? Honesty? What's that? I'm crazy and just say random things that are outrageous and wacky! Guess what scene partner? For no reason at all I'm going to say you're fucking a donkey! This is great!"

The situation is immediately absurd – all of the characters instantly are insane homeless people who are simultaneously hooked on crack and opera singers who each have a three-legged pet zebra. *Wacky ≠ funny*. Trust yourself that you are smart enough, funny enough, and talented enough to do an honest, truthful, grounded scene. That doesn't mean your scene can't be weird or take a strange turn, but it can't start that way. If you start crazy then we have nothing to grab onto – there has to be some sort of base reality. You are much better starting off with a fully grounded scene that isn't funny and exploring it (I guarantee it will turn into one of the funniest scenes you ever do). Stop trying to be funny and react honestly and play truthfully. Treat the scene and relationship with the same honesty and integrity you treat your off-stage relationships. Let's all do our part to take Wacky Town, USA off the map. Be truthful and honest in scenes (and in advertising – please stop advertising your shows as "wacky," "zany," or any other synonym that implies men will be dressed as ballerinas and women will have crazy mismatched pigtails in neon scrunchies).

A Word About Walk-Ons, Off-Stage Characters, and Other "Tricks"

Don't do them. Unless they are absolutely necessary. For instance, a walk-on that helps answer "why you two, why now?", or if a character is called onto stage. If you do use them, use them sparingly. Nothing will

63

ruin a good scene or set faster than a team falling in love with walk-ons or back-line interference. Your job with a walk-on or extra or whatever is to aid and heighten the scene, not hijack it with your great idea. An appropriate and well-timed walk-on can really benefit a scene. Too many can kill your show.

Some Words About Being Stuck In Your Head

One of the most common phrases amongst improvisers is "I'm stuck in my head." This is generally meant as a negative comment, referencing the fact that you are thinking too hard and not playing and reacting. Being stuck in your head isn't necessarily a bad thing. As a student of improv, you will be stuck in your head. It is part of the learning process. Being stuck in your head means you are thinking about all of the rules and maxims and don'ts that we just described. It means you are paying attention and getting better.

The end goal is that you practice enough and improvise enough so you get to the point where you don't have to think about rules and maxims because they are second nature. And even then you will go through patches where you get stuck in your head. Usually these periods are the times where you emerge better at improv than you were before you got stuck in your head. There is a lot to think about on stage, so it's okay to be stuck in your head. There are good times to be stuck in your head – like when you realize you are bulldozing a scene and need to let your partner talk, or you realize you have no relationship, or that you are at a different locale than your scene partner. It isn't helpful to be stuck in your head because you are worried about messing up. Or you notice that you haven't been in many scenes, so you jump in one "just because," or say a joke because "I'm not getting any laughs." Or think, "I need to save this scene."

Anytime you learn something new, the component parts can seem difficult. Riding a bike, driving a car, or learning how to knit all have a lot of moving parts that work in concert, just like improv. As with any of those tasks, at the beginning it's difficult to manage them all. You have to concentrate on working those knitting needles, paying very close attention to each and every stitch. With practice, these tasks become second nature. My wife can knit a hat while having a full-blown intellectual conversation. She doesn't have to look at the needles. It's like her hands are acting independently. Improv, with practice, can become second nature. But you need to go through periods where you are in your head thinking about what you are doing so that you can grow and move on to periods where you are simply playing in the moment.

What will be easy and difficult varies from person to person. You will catch on to certain ideas very quickly and others will stymie you. There isn't a right or wrong way to progress through improv. You will experience moments of complete playfulness while your partner is stuck in his head, and vice versa. Don't get too worried about being stuck in your head; simply focus on getting better and know that being stuck is part of the process.

Notes

1 If you are a Knicks fan, I'm sorry for bringing up his name. If it makes you feel better, as a Bulls fan it still boils my blood that he walked off the court in the 1991 Eastern Conference Finals.
2 Repeating something within a scene is also the Chicago definition of "game." See "The Game of the Scene" for more info.
3 Charna Halpern, Del Close, and Kim "Howard" Johnson. *Truth in Comedy: The Manual of Improvisation*. Colorado Springs, CO: Meriwether Publishing, 1994, 15.
4 Halpern, Close, and Johnson, 63.
5 Keith Johnstone. *Impro: Improvisation and the Theatre*. New York: Routledge, 1989, 87–8.
6 Mick Napier. *Improvise: Scene From the Inside Out*. Portsmouth, NH: Heinemann, 2004, 14, 16.
7 For years Johnstone's *Impro* was the only improv book Close recommended to students.
8 Side note: Stop rushing through your object work. Take your time and actually do it. It not only helps bring honesty to your scene, it also keeps you from having to invent. If you change the tire in 9 seconds, now you have to find something else to do. Play what's there. As long as we are on the topic of object work, remember that **how** you do something is more important than **what** you do. Building a fire with great care is different than just throwing some twigs on a flame – those are two very different characters. Put the how before the what.
9 That doesn't mean improv should become your therapy. It isn't where you work out your problems and emotional issues. It simply means that you should play what's there. Go read Jimmy Carrane's *Improv Therapy: How to Get Out of Your Own Way to Become a Better Improviser* to get some tools to deal with and use your emotions, feelings, thoughts, etc. on stage.

Skill Building
Exercises

If you want to be good at improv, no matter what genre or style, you have to be able to do a good scene. And if you want to be good at scene work, you need to rehearse. These exercises and warm-ups are compiled from a wide array of improv schools and philosophies (and a few of our own... though pretty much everything here is either from Viola Spolin or adapted from Viola Spolin, or a Viola Spolin exercise that somebody unconsciously recreated). They are designed to help you do good scene work. If you can do a good two-person scene, you can do any genre or style of improv that you want. The following warm-ups and exercises are meant to introduce and hone specific skills necessary for solid scene work, but not necessarily meant for performance (of course you can always try). This list contains a number of exercises that we've found helpful in our experience working with collegiate improvisers. Though they are categorized, many warm-ups and exercises work multiple skill sets. For instance, nearly any game we have classified as Energy/Physicality also improves Group Mind. As you can guess, this list is hardly exhaustive, so please continue to search for new games and exercises ... or pull a Spolin and make up your own!

Warm-Ups

- **Energy/Physicality**
  - Energy Pass
  - Shake Out
  - Whoosh
  - Zip-Zap-Zop
  - Bippity-Bippity-Bop
  - Big Booty
  - Do You Like Your Neighbor?
  - Kitty Want A Corner?
  - Cat and Mouse
  - Enemy/Protector
  - Ants on a Cracker
  - Cars
  - 1–10 Walking
  - Lead Walking
  - Slow Motion Race
  - Get Up Like Logan
  - Dance Your Dance
  - Contact Improvisation
    - Clay Sculpting Game
    - Banana Rolls (Crescent Rolls)
    - Basic Rolling Contact

- **Improv Muscle**
  - Sound Ball
  - Word Association
  - Ba-DaDa
  - Machine
  - Heightening Game
  - Emotional Build
  - Oscar Moment
  - Prince of Paris
  - What Are You Doing?
  - Red Ball
  - Spaghetti
  - Tic-Toc
  - Would You Like to Buy a Duck?
  - Box Game
  - Opening Pathways

- **Group Mind**
  - Pass the Clap
  - Counting
  - Skip 3's
  - 1, 2, 3 People Walking
  - Run to the Middle
  - Caligula

68

Exercises

- Group Mind
  - Seven Things
  - Patterns
  - A–C Patterns
  - Mind Meld
  - Hot Spot
- Physicality/Object Work
  - Environmental Support
  - Loaf of Bread
  - Realtor
  - Counter Circles
- Agreement
  - Yes, And
  - Yes, Let's
  - Ad Game
  - Crisis Situation
- Initiating Scenes
  - The Zero Line
  - Initiations
  - Goalie
  - Three-Line Scenes
  - Four-Line Scenes
  - Heat and Weight
  - Silent Connection
- Building Scenes
  - A–B
  - Color/Advance
  - Repetition
  - That's Important to Me
  - Solo Character Switches
  - One Actor, Two Characters
  - Three-Way Conversation
  - Give and Take
  - Master–Servant
  - Status Party
  - Status Swap
  - Crutch Dialogue
  - Back-To-Back Chairs
  - Freeze
  - I Remember …

Warm-Ups

Energy/Physicality

Exercise: Energy Pass

Description: The entire group forms a circle. One person begins by making a sound and movement. The person to the right immediately repeats the sound and movement, and so on all the way around the circle. After the movement/sound goes all the way around the circle, the next person in line (the person who first repeated the sound/movement) performs a new sound/movement that makes its way around the circle. This continues until everyone in the circle has initiated a sound/movement. As you can tell, speed is imperative, both to build energy and to keep the game moving.

Skills: Group Mind, "Yes, And", Initiations ... and Energy of course.

Teaching Tips: Remember to receive the energy before passing it to the next person. And keep it FAST!

Exercise: Shake Out

Description: The entire group forms a circle. Starting with an eight count, in unison each player "shakes" out a particular body part. One circuit contains eight "shakes" of the right arm, then the left arm, right leg, left leg, and finally the whole body. The process repeats, but is cut in half – so four "shakes" on the next circuit, two on the next, and finally one on the last circuit. You can also simply go 8, 7, 6, 5, 4, 3, 2, 1 instead of using halves.

Skills: Physicality, Group Mind.

Teaching Tips: Players should count with a strong voice, and should make eye contact with the other players in the circle. The energy and tempo need to remain high.

Exercise: Whoosh

Description: This can be played with any number, though smaller does tend to keep the pace quicker. There are several moves within the game.

1. Whoosh: As though you are passing all of the energy in the world in a tidal wave, you turn to the person next to you and say "Whoosh!" Initially the Whoosh should move in the same

direction, but as the game goes on it can go in either direction or be passed across the circle.

2. Oil Slick: If a player says "Oil Slick," the Whoosh then skips a player and is picked up by the next. An Oil Slick can be repeated, so you can oil slick an oil slick.

3. Ramp: If a player says "Ramp," the next two players jump in unison, and the third player picks up the Whoosh.

4. Bridge: If a player says "Bridge," the next two must duck or crouch down in unison, and the third player picks up the Whoosh.

Skills: Energy, Attentiveness, and Group Mind.

Teaching Tips: Keep up the pace, and don't be afraid to let a new rule organically emerge.

Exercise: Zip-Zap-Zop

Description: Any number of players in a circle. Any person makes eye contact with another and clap-points while saying "Zip." Immediately that person must turn to another, make eye contact, clap-point and say "Zap." The next player follows the same guidelines and says "Zop." Players continue passing the "Zip-Zap-Zop" while maintaining the beat. You can play this as an elimination game. If someone messes up the rhythm or pattern or makes an unclear pass, they are out.

Skills: Focus, Group Mind, Keeping a Rhythm, Being Present, and Diction.

Teaching Tips: It's not about winning the game; it's about passing the energy. Focus on clear and crisp passes and keep up the pace.

Exercise: Bippity-Bippity-Bop

Description: 8–12 players form a circle, with one player in the middle. The player in the middle's goal is to get out of the middle. They have three tools to do so. 1) Approach any player, make eye contact, and say "Bippity-bippity-bop." The other player must say "Bop" before the player in the middle finishes saying "Bippity-bippity-bop." 2) Approach any player, make eye contact, and say "Bop." In this case, the other player must be silent. If he or she says anything or makes any noise, he or she moves to the middle. 3) Point at any player and instruct them to become something specific (a place, noun, person, etc.). The player and the person on the

71

right and left must work as a unit to physically create the item, person, etc., before the player in the middle counts to five. For example, if I point at you and say "Palm tree!", you can stand up straight with your arms in the air and the people on your right and left form palm leaves. If any of the three players fails to accomplish the task, they move to the middle.

Skills: Listening, Awareness, Spontaneity, Energy, Diction, and Physicality.

Teaching Tips: Remember to keep up the pace. The person in the middle should be moving quickly, both to keep up the energy and as a strategy to get out of the middle.

Exercise: Big Booty

Description: 8–12 players form a circle. One player becomes Big Booty while the others count off, starting with the player to the left of Big Booty. The game always begins with everyone saying "Aw shit, Big Booty Big Booty. Big Booty Big Booty Big Booty." This establishes the tempo to be followed for the rest of the game. Here is an example of the call and response.

```
All players: "Aw shit (or "Aw yeah" if you don't
    want to curse), Big Booty. Big Booty. Big
    Booty Big Booty Big Booty."
Big Booty: "Big Booty, Number One."
Number One: "Number One, Number Seven."
Number Seven: "Number Seven, Number Four."
Number Four: "Number Four, Big Booty."
Big Booty: "Big Booty, Number Nine." And so on.
```

During the call and response, if someone breaks rhythm, says the wrong number, responds to the wrong number, or doesn't respond in time for their own number, they must enter the middle of the circle and dance. During the dance, they must make their way to the right of Big Booty, becoming the last number in the circle. All other players shift their numbers accordingly, but the game does not stop. This happens while everyone resets by saying, "Aw shit, Big Booty Big Booty. Big Booty Big Booty Big Booty." If Big Booty messes up, they too must dance in the middle of the circle and become the last number in the formation. Number One now becomes Big Booty.

Skills: Group Mind, Listening, Rhythm, and Focus.

Teaching Tips: Failing is inevitable, and is part of the game. Learning how to make mistakes is an essential component of improv. Keep the beat and make sure it flows, which is more important than winning.

Exercise: Do You Like Your Neighbor?

Description: The entire group forms a circle with one person in the middle. The person in the middle will go up to another player and say "Do you like your neighbor?" That player may reply with either "Yes" or "No." If the player says "No" the two people on either side of that player must quickly switch spots before the person in the middle steals one of their spots. If the player says "Yes," they must then name a general (non-physical) quality that they don't like. For example, a player might say "Yes, but I don't like people who pee in the shower." This means that anyone in the circle who pees in the shower must quickly find a new spot in the circle until someone is left in the middle.

Skills: Listening, Energy, Physicality, and Honesty.

Teaching Tips: Make sure there is enough room for this exercise. Keep up the pace and be honest with yourself and the people around you!

Exercise: Kitty Want A Corner?

Description: In this classic Viola Spolin exercise, 8–16 players form a rectangle or square. One person is in the middle. The person in the middle can approach any player and ask them "Kitty want a corner?" The player then responds, "Go ask your neighbor." These are the only two things said in the game. While this is happening, the other players must make eye contact with one another and then switch positions (non-verbally). If the player in the middle finds an opening in the rectangle/square, the player left out of the configuration is now in the middle. Think Duck, Duck, Goose. If the player in the middle can count to five without anyone switching places, he or she can select any player to be in the middle.

Skills: Energy, Non-Verbal Communication, Awareness (spatial and otherwise), Trusting Your Partner, and Cardio.

Teaching Tips: Make sure there is ample space and you aren't by any walls or things people can fall off or into. Keep up the pace!

Exercise: Cat and Mouse

Description: 6+ players. One player is the "cat" and one player is the "mouse." The other players find a partner and lock arms (if there is an odd number, there can be a group of three). The cat simply tries to catch the mouse. The mouse can latch onto any group by locking arms with one of the players. The player not latched onto is released and becomes the new mouse. If the cat catches the mouse, the players switch roles and the chase continues.

Skills: Energy and Team Building.

Teaching Tips: The game is all about energy, so keep up the pace. Make people aware of their surroundings to avoid injury.

Exercise: Enemy/Protector

Description: 6+ players. Each player picks someone else in the ensemble who is his or her enemy. Players also pick another player to be their protector. Do not share who is your enemy or your protector. When the leader says "Go," your sole job is to keep your protector between you and your enemy. That's it. Seems simple, but it can become very physical and move very quickly if your entire ensemble is playing.

Skills: Energy and Team Building.

Teaching Tips: Again, this game is about energy and movement. Don't try to cheat the game by standing in the corner or something of that ilk. Let loose and play. At the end of the game it's also fun to see who picked whom to be their enemy and protector.

Exercise: Ants on a Cracker

Description: This exercise from 500 Clown can use as many players as you'd like, but it must be an *odd* number. Begin by having players walk around the room imagining that they are ants walking on top of a cracker that is floating in a giant glass of milk. The group must keep the cracker balanced so that it doesn't fall into the milk. Players must fill negative space and be aware of the overall spacing of the group. As the game progresses, make the players move faster to the point where players are running. Then, make them partner up. One player will be left without a partner. Instruct the rest of the group to move away from that individual and look at them. The coach (or other outsider) asks the loner how they feel. Some version of "Shitty" is said, and the exercise continues with all of the ants moving about the space again. The coach then instructs the ants to partner up several more times.

Skills: Physicality, Awareness, and Soft Focus.

Teaching Tips: As the game progresses, players will become more invested for fear of being left isolated. The idea is to let the real emotions you are feeling affect you. You are tired, afraid, experiencing an adrenaline rush – feel these things in the moment and remember how they affected you so that you can feel them again and let them affect you again on stage. A true, real, and honest emotional reaction/ discovery on stage is worth its weight in gold.

Exercise: Cars

Description: Can be done with any amount of players. Players pair up. One is the "car" and one is the "driver." The car closes his or her eyes. The driver stands behind the car and will non-verbally steer. The rules for driving are as follows:

- To go forward, the driver slides his or her index finger up the car's back.
- To go in reverse, the driver slides his or her index finger down the car's back.
- To go right or left, the driver slides his or her index finger right or left.
- To go faster, the driver increases pressure.
- To go slower, the driver decreases pressure.
- To stop, the driver removes his or her finger.
- The only time the driver can speak is if there is immediate danger.

75

The driver then drives the car around the room trying to avoid other cars. After a set time, switch roles.

Skills: Trust, Support Your Partner, and Focus.

Teaching Tips: Strictly enforce the no-talking policy. Some people will be more comfortable with their eyes closed than others. That's okay, but don't let them off the hook. Keep an eye out for collisions.

Exercise: 1–10 Walking

Description: Any number of players. Players simply begin walking about the room (going in a circle or back and forth works). The leader will introduce the intensity scale from 1, which is very low energy, to 10, which is very high energy, with 5 being a sort of neutral. Players should start at a 5. At various points the leader will call out a new number and players will adjust their energy and intensity. The leader can introduce other variables as well, such as age, occupation, status, body type, etc.

Skills: Physicality, Space Work, Character Development, and Walking.

Teaching Tips: Make sure players differentiate between like numbers. They should be able to show you (and tell you) the difference between a 7 and 8, or 2 and 3, not just a 2 and 8.

Exercise: Lead Walking

Description: Any number of players. Players simply begin walking about the room (going in a circle or back and forth works). At various times the leader will instruct the players to lead with a particular body part ("Lead with your foot." "Lead with your forehead." "Lead with your pelvis.").

Skills: Physicality, Space Work, Character Development, and Walking.

Teaching Tips: This game is similar to 1–10 Walking and the exercises can be combined if desired.

Exercise: Slow Motion Race

Description: A famous Augusto Boal exercise that can work with any number of players, but it can be helpful to break into smaller groups. Players line up as though they are running a race. In this race, however, the slowest runner wins. The only two rules are: 1) You must always be moving forward, and 2) You must take long strides.

Skills: Physicality, Gag Your Inner Critic.

Teaching Tips: While it is a race, winning isn't as important as understanding your muscles. The game is designed to show players how much control they have (or don't) over their bodies. Therefore, taking long strides is imperative because it is more physically demanding. Players will also go much too fast the first time they do this exercise. Really push them to move as slow as they possibly can. It isn't that hard to "pretend" to go slow, but it is highly physically demanding (and revealing) to actually go as slow as possible.

Exercise: Get Up Like Logan

Description: Any number of players. Everyone starts by lying on the floor. When the leader says, "Get up like Logan!", everyone must get up in the most cumbersome, strenuously difficult way imaginable, preferably in circles. There are three rules: 1) you must get up as slowly as possible; 2) you must **always** be moving; and 3) you must complain the entire time. The leader then says, "Sit down!" and everyone must sit as quickly as possible. This cycle then repeats for as long as you'd like, preferably altering the way that you get up each time.

Skills: Energy, Physicality, Spontaneity, and Character Development.

Teaching Tips: Take your time getting up. Don't rush the process. While you should be constantly moving, it isn't a race to see who can get up fastest. As a matter of fact, it is the exact opposite. Notice how different physical movements can alter your mindset, and think about how that might be applied to character development.

Exercise: Dance Your Dance

Description: Any number of players forms a circle. One player enters the circle and begins a movement-based dance using the entire circle. At some point the dancer will go up to another player in the circle and the two will begin sharing the dance. The second player then takes the dance into the circle and organically transforms it in some way into his or her own dance. The same pattern continues until all players have danced.

Skills: Physicality, Support Your Partner, Agreement, Gag Your Inner Critic, and "Yes, And".

Teaching Tips: Let the dancers take some time in the middle. Undoubtedly several players will try to get out of the middle as quickly as possible, but push them to try and make a new discovery. Don't preplan your dance – take what you are given and see what organically emerges.

Exercise: Contact Improvisation

Contact improvisation is a form of dance where points of physical contact serve as the starting point for physical movement and exploration. The principles can be useful to comic improvisation, or to simply enhance your movement or physicality. So here are a few exercises that can help you explore contact improvisation.

77

EXERCISE: CLAY SCULPTING GAME

Description: Players break into pairs; one is the sculptor and the other is the clay. The sculptor then gently moves the clay's body parts to mold the clay into an artistic shape. For example, you might have your partner point at something across the room and then animate his or her face into excitement or fear. Then ask the sculptor to create five more interesting sculptures. The more they are forced to do, the better they will become and the less obvious the sculptures will become (you'll get less nose picking sculptures). Have players switch roles and repeat the exercise. Then, have the sculptor use five steps to manipulate the clay into a shape or position. The clay must remember each step because the clay must then recreate the movement without the sculptor. The final position is not nearly as important as careful and accurately performing the steps of getting there. Have the players repeat several times, switching roles throughout. You can then have the players combine several movements into a short scenic motif between the two players.

Skills: Physicality, Movement, Gagging Your Inner Critic, and Support Your Partner.

Teaching Tips: The quality and precision of movement is much more important than creating a funny scene or making your partner do something silly.

EXERCISE: BANANA ROLLS (CRESCENT ROLLS)

Description: Players lie on the floor and take the shape of a crescent moon or banana. Each player then begins rolling while the body maintains a crescent shape. So your back is alternately extending or flexing (so the banana or crescent should look the same whether you are facing forward or looking backward).

Skills: Physicality and Movement.

Teaching Tips: Really focus on keeping the shape consistent as you move. Feel how your body has to shift, how your muscles relax or tense as you roll.

EXERCISE: BASIC ROLLING CONTACT

Description: With a partner, explore contact improvisation movement on the floor (rolling). Explore various points of contact, exchanging weight, and counterbalancing one another. Stay on the ground, as this is the most basic and safest way to explore. Really focus on moving in harmony. Practice your physical listening skills – listen for what your partner wants from you by feeling how he or she is moving.

Skills: Physicality, Movement, Gagging Your Inner Critic, "Yes, And", and Support Your Partner.

Teaching Tips: This might feel weird. But it is a great way to build physicality into your group, as well as building trust. Don't focus on doing it right or wrong; focus on responding to what your partner needs/wants in the moment (which if you think about it is all that improv really is anyway).

79

Improv Muscle

Exercise: Sound Ball

Description: Form a circle. This can be done with as many or as few players as you'd like. One person starts with an imaginary ball. To pass the ball, he or she must make eye contact with another player and then make a sound while "throwing" the ball. To catch the ball, the receiving player must mimic the throwing player's sound (so if Player 1 says "Ohhhhhh" when he throws the ball, Player 2 must say "Ohhhhhh" when she catches the ball). This continues for several minutes. The ball should move quickly and without hesitation.

Skills: Group Mind, Spontaneity, Gag Your Inner Critic, Listening, Energy, Opening Yourself Up to Receive, and Eye Contact.

Teaching Tips: Make sure the pace is fast and that nobody is pausing when they get the ball. Players should catch and throw very quickly so that they don't have time to judge what sound they are going to make. Try to avoid using actual words and make players stick to making sounds. Make sure they are being specific about who they are passing the ball to – both through direct eye contact and by giving a clear and specific pass and sound.

Exercise: Word Association

Description: Form a circle or horseshoe with 6–10 players. One player will start by simply saying a word. In no particular order another player will say the first word that pops into his or her head. And so on. For example:

Player 1: Potato
Player 2: Famine
Player 3: Hunger
Player 4: Nachos
Player 5: Cheese
Player 3: Camera
Player 2: Wedding
Player 1: Groom
Player 5: Hair

Another variation is to form a circle with 6–10 players. One player goes in the middle. That player stands face to face with another player, who says a word to the player in the middle. The player in the middle then free-associates around the circle as quickly as possible. The same premise applies as above (say the first thing that pops into your head), but this variation gives a bit of order to the association and puts more weight on one player. When that player makes it all the way around the circle (this should be fast), the next player (the one who gave the initial first word) steps into the middle. Continue until all players have been in the middle.

Skills: Group Mind, Gagging Your Inner Critic, Spontaneity, and Originality.

Teaching Tips: Remember to keep the game fast. Don't allow players to take time to think of what to say – the whole point is to simply respond.

*A note about word association. It is great for building group mind, getting out of your head, and warming up. It is pretty toxic during a scene. You don't want to simply use word association in a scene because that will often lead you to stray from the trunk of your scene. In a scene make sure you focus on the heart of the scene.

Exercise: Ba-DaDa

Description: 6–12 players stand in a circle. This is a variation of word association that comes from UCB. The players start a rhythm by clapping and then slapping their thighs. In rhythm player 1 says a word, to which player 2 responds, again in rhythm. Then the entire group repeats the two words and says "Ba-DaDa." For example:

Player 1: Apple
Player 2: Chair
ALL: Apple Chair Ba-DaDa.

Player 2 then says another word to start the next association.

Player 2: Wood
Player 3: Carpenter
ALL: Wood Carpenter Ba-DaDa.

And so on.

Skills: Group Mind, Gagging Your Inner Critic, Spontaneity, Listening, and Originality.

Teaching Tips: Stay on beat. Keeping the rhythm going is as important as anything. You can also speed the rhythm up as you go to keep players on their toes.

Exercise: Machine

Description: 6–12 players form a back line. One player steps onstage and begins a repetitive motion and sound. A second player complements this action by making his or her own repetitive motion and sound. A third joins in and so on until all of the players are together onstage. The players all continue their motions and sounds, either increasing or decreasing the speed of "the machine" as a unit. Once the machine is built, any player can jump out of the machine, start a new movement and sound and then the team builds a new machine.

Skills: Group Mind, Physicality, Listening, Support Your Partner, and "Yes, And".

Teaching Tips: Don't take too much time between players. While you don't want everyone jumping in at the same time, the machine should be built relatively quickly. Really focus on complementing what has been built and adding a necessary component.

Exercise: Heightening Game

Description: 6–10 players form a circle. One player steps into the middle and says a word. As quickly as possible another player steps into the middle and replaces the original player by saying a word that heightens or tops the original. This continues for several minutes. For example:

Player 1: Bread
Player 2: Toast with butter
Player 3: Fried egg on toast
Player 4: A chicken
Player 5: A fox
Player 6: A British lord
Player 3: The king
Player 2: Democracy
Player 4: Voter fraud

Skills: Group Mind, Heightening, Spontaneity, Support Your Partner, Gag Your Inner Critic, and Listening.

Teaching Tips: Keep the game fast – no one should be in the middle for more than a second or two. Make sure players are heightening the previous word rather than just doing word association. The trick is to get them to trust themselves even if they don't have a heightened word in mind – you cannot leave the person in the middle too long, otherwise the game dies.

Exercise: Emotional Build

Description: 6 players form a line. The first player says a line and performs a basic gesture. He or she does this with minimum emotional investment (like a 3 on a 1–10 emotional investment scale). The next player takes that gesture and line and turns up the emotional and physical investment. This process repeats until the last player delivers a 10 (or higher) on the emotional and physical investment scale.

Skills: Emotional Point of View, Physicality, Heightening, and Character Development.

Teaching Tips: The whole point of the game is to show the power of emotional and physical investment. While you wouldn't always start a scene at a 10, it can sometimes be a powerful tool. That said, starting with a strong emotional and physical point of view is a solid way to begin any scene. Likewise, understanding how to build a character or emotion in a scene is always useful.

Exercise: Oscar Moment

Description: 2 players perform a basic scene. At a given point in the scene, the leader will call out to one of the players, "This is your Oscar moment!" Said player then delivers an Oscar-worthy monologue that reveals background information, deepens the relationship, and clearly defines his or her intentions. The scene then resumes until the leader calls out to the other player, "This is your Oscar moment!" and the other player delivers a similar monologue. The players then bring the scene to an end.

Skills: Character Development, Scene Development, Emotional Point of View, Support Your Partner, Spontaneity, and Agreement.

Teaching Tips: Do your best to avoid generic cheese. Not at the store, because I buy generic cheese, but in the sense that the monologue is not meant to be a moment where you fake cry. It is meant to help deepen the relationship and situation. It is a moment to reveal information that heightens the game, raises the stakes, and clarifies your intentions.

Exercise: Prince of Paris

Description: 8–16 players stand in a straight line facing the leader. Players number themselves 1, 2, 3, etc.. The leader then begins the game by saying, "The Prince of Paris lost his hat, Number X knows where it's at." The player with the corresponding number takes

83

one step forward and replies, "Who sir, me sir?" The entire call and response is below:

```
Leader: "The Prince of Paris lost his hat,
    Number 1 knows where it's at."
Number 1: "Who sir, me sir?"
Leader: "Yes sir, you sir."
Number 1: "No, not I sir."
Leader: "Well then, who sir?"
Number 1: "Number 5, sir."
Number 5 (takes one step forward): "Who sir, me
    sir?"
*This must be said before the leader can say
    "Number 5, you're out."
Leader: "Yes sir, you sir."
Number 5: "No, not I sir."
Leader: "Well then, who sir?"
Number 5: "Number 2, sir."
```

84

Players are out if they stumble over their lines, or if the leader can call them out due to a delay. Players to the right of the ousted player shift down one number. So if I am Number 6, and Number 5 is called out, I now become Number 5, the person on my right Number 6, and so on. The game, however, does not stop. There is no formal re-counting; each player is responsible for the changes that happen throughout the game. If the leader happens to falter, they are out and Number 1 becomes the new leader.

Skills: Focus, Listening, Getting Out of Your Head, and Being in the Moment.

Teaching Tips: Don't be nice – feel free to kick people out of the game. If there is a discrepancy about numbers, it is at the leader's discretion. Remember that the flow of the game is more important than an individual's desire to win.

Exercise: What Are You Doing?

Description: Any number of players forms two lines. One player starts to perform an activity. The next person in line asks, "What are you doing?" The first player then responds with an activity that they are not performing. For example, the first player is brushing their hair and the second asks, "What are you doing?" The response might be,

"Fighting a bear." The second player must then imitate that action. When asked by the next person, "What are you doing?", they must respond with another activity as well, and so on.

Skills: Spontaneity, Space Work, Listening, Physicality, and Accepting Ideas.

Teaching Tips: Keep an eye out for similar activities to make sure they are varied. Encourage 100% investment in your giving activity.

Exercise: Red Ball

Description: 6–12 players in a circle (more can work as well). You can play this game with real colored balls or you can pantomime the balls. One player starts with the Red Ball. They make eye contact with someone, and ask them "Red Ball?" That player responds with "Red Ball." At that point the first player physically passes the ball. This continues with no set sequence or pattern. At some point a Blue Ball is introduced. Players should continue passing the Red Ball. The action is the same, except players ask "Blue Ball?" and respond with "Blue Ball." Add as many balls as you would like to the game.

Skills: Listening, Focus, Connection and Eye Contact, Making Yourself Available and Open, Awareness, and Group Mind.

Teaching Tips: Let players establish a rhythm/pattern before introducing a new ball that will alter/break that pattern. Make sure to stress that making yourself available to receive a pass is as important to the success of the game as anything – players should never be disconnected or idle.

Exercise: Spaghetti

Description: 6–12 players form a circle. The first pass is Spaghetti. One player makes direct eye contact with another player, offers them an imaginary bowl, and says, "Spaghetti?" The player receives the bowl and says, "Maybe tomorrow." Note: This can be done with or without a terrible Italian accent.

The second pass is Ninja. One player will make direct eye contact with another player, pantomime throwing a dagger, and yell "Die!" The other player will clap his or her hands together as though catching the imaginary dagger and say "Not today." Note: You always catch the dagger. Players then pass the dagger around the circle in this manner. Once Ninja is established, then reintroduce Spaghetti and have both going at the same time.

The third pass is Hawk. One player will make direct eye contact with another player, and hold his or her arm out as though a hawk is resting on his or her forearm, and say, "Hawk?" The other player places his or her arm out to receive the hawk and says, "Come, Hawk." Once this is established, the other two passes can be re-introduced so that eventually all three passes are happening simultaneously.

Skills: Listening, Focus, Connection and Eye Contact, Making Yourself Available and Open, Awareness, and Group Mind.

Teaching Tips: Introduce each new element slowly, and feel free to make up three of your own elements. Again, stress that making yourself available to receive a pass is as important to the success of the game as anything. In improv you aren't just giving information; you must be open to receive as well.

Exercise: Tic-Toc

Description: Players form a circle. This can be done with any number, but for time's sake it might be best with 10–12. One person is the Control and they have two objects; one is called a Tic, the other a Toc (the objects can be anything but should be small so they can be easily passed between people). The Control turns to the player on his or her right, hands them the Tic object and says: "This is a Tic." That player responds, "A what?" Control replies, "A Tic." Player 1: "Oh, a Tic." Player 1 then turns to the person on his or her right and says, "This is a Tic." Player 2 responds, "A what?" At this point Player 1 turns back to Control and asks "A what?" Control responds with "A Tic." Player 1 then says to Player 2 "A Tic." Player 2 says, "Oh, a Tic." He or she turns to Player 3 and repeats the sequence. Every time the "A what?" section goes all the way back to the Control player. While this is happening, the Control player turns to the player on his or her left, hands them the Toc object and says, "This is a Toc." The same progression happens as with the Tic side, only substitute Toc for Tic. The game will be fairly smooth initially, but when the Tic and Toc cross one another (roughly this will happen to the folks across the circle from the Control player), things will get messy and players must really focus.

Skills: Focus, Listening, Control What You Can Control, Group Mind, and Communication.

Teaching Tips: Let the group flounder if things get messy (if things get messy right away, review the rules and make sure the group understands the basic transaction and lines). Let them yell at one another and blame one another and get frustrated.

Exercise: Would You Like to Buy a Duck?

Description: A variant of Tic-Toc, this game should be played with 6–12 players who form a circle. Each player in turn will ask the player to his or her right, "Would you like to buy a _____?" The player on the right will ask a question specific to the item, "Does it _____?" All other dialogue is scripted per the below:

```
Player 1: "Would you like to buy a duck?"
    (*Player 1 always begins with a duck.)
Player 2: "A what?"
Player 1: "A duck."
Player 2: "Does it quack?"
Player 1: "Of course it quacks."
Player 2: "Then I'll buy it."
Player 1: "Good."
Player 2: "Would you like to buy a shoe?"
Player 3: "A what?"
Player 2: (to Player 1): "A what?" (*As with
    Tic-Toc, the "A what?" goes all the way
    back to Player 1.)
Player 1: "A duck."
Player 2: "A shoe." (*You always reply with your
    item.)
Player 3: "Does it fit?"
Player 2: "Does it quack?"
Player 1: "Of course it quacks."
Player 2: "Of course it fits." (*Again, you
    always reply with your item.)
Player 3: "Then I'll buy it."
Player 2: (to Player 1) "Then I'll buy it."
Player 1: "Good."
Player 2: "Good."
```

And so on …

If you are brave, you can go around the circle a second time. If that is the case, you must still reference the first go 'round. So the "A what?" would go around the circle twice, then each player would repeat his or her first item/question before getting to the second. Mind. Explosion!

Teaching Tips: This game is a step up in difficulty from Tic-Toc …
and players will undoubtedly struggle initially. Help them through
it. Remind them that all they really have to remember is one item
(which they named) and one question about the item given to them
(which they asked). All other dialogue is scripted.

Exercise: Box Game

Description: Any number of players, put into pairs. One player is
holding an imaginary box, and they are trying to state what is inside.
The other player simply says, "No" to whatever is said. For example:

```
1: It's a bunny.
2: No.
1: It's a piñata.
2: No.
1: It's a chair.
2: No.
1: It's world peace.
2: No.
1: It's blue.
2: No.
```

And so on, until eventually Player 2 says, "Yes."
Skills: Spontaneity, Originality, and Slow Comedy.
Teaching Tips: The game is designed to be frustrating and a bit
discouraging. That's okay, because the goal is to get players beyond
their stock answers and to push into new and unexpected territories.
It's always nice to play "Yes, And" after this game.

Exercise: Opening Pathways

Description: These exercises came to me through Jill Bernard and can
be done as individuals, or within the group. The whole concept is to
experience things anew. As an adult your neural pathways tend to be
pretty set and we do our best not to experience things in new ways. As
a child, everything is new to you. So these are simple exercises meant
to help you see things anew again and to open up those pathways.

- Walk around your room and give things different names. Your
  desk is now a portario. Your computer a lassar. Your bed a fork.
  This will be really difficult at first. Keep pushing.

88

- Spin around really fast with your eyes closed. Stop and open your eyes. Focus directly in front of you and imagine that what you are seeing (with blurred lines and swirling images) is exactly how it is supposed to look. Take it in as a new thing. Examine it. Understand it. Think about how weird a chair must look to a baby.
- Do common tasks with your off hand. Brush your teeth or hair lefty (or righty). Button your shirt the opposite way you normally do. Tie your shoes the opposite way. Normal tasks will suddenly be a lot harder and you'll think about the component steps more.
- Find a new route to walk to your classes every day for a month. If you go the same way and see the same things every day, you stop paying attention.
- Open up a notebook. Pick up a pen. Write for five minutes straight. Do not stop. Do not worry if you are only writing the letter "r" over and over. Five minutes is a long time. Push yourself.

Skills: Spontaneity, Gag Your Inner Critic, Make Active Choices, and Commitment.

Teaching Tips: There are limitless variations on this exercise. The main idea is to get you to experience things in a new way. You need to be flexible in improv, and these types of exercises are immensely helpful in making you a better performer.

Group Mind

Exercise: Pass the Clap

Description: This can be played with any number, though smaller does tend to keep the pace quicker. The first player turns to the player on his or her right; they make eye contact and then clap in unison. The clap then makes its way around the circle in this manner. Once the rhythm has been established, a player can reverse the flow by clapping in unison and then maintaining eye contact with the same player and clapping again in unison (in rhythm). A player can pass the clap across the circle by making eye contact with any player and clapping in unison (and maintaining the rhythm).

Skills: Group Mind, Rhythm, Awareness, Focus, and Clapping.

Teaching Tips: The rhythm is the most important element. Changing direction or any other variation should only occur if the group maintains the rhythm. Players who tend to have issues listening in scenes tend to force changes of direction – this is a helpful spot to point out that the rhythm of the clap is more important than personal whims, much like the success of a scene is more important than a joke or an individual's wants.

Exercise: Counting

Description: 3–12 players form a circle. You can play with your eyes opened or closed (if the group isn't particularly focused, eyes closed can be helpful). Working as a group, players try and count as high as possible (the number of players doesn't limit the numbers counted – go as high as possible). The only rule is that only one player can speak at a time. So if three people all say "Four" at the same time the group would have to go back and start at one. While it isn't technically against the rules, forming a basic pattern such as simply going in order around the circle is sort of cheating. If numbers scare you or you want a tangible end goal, you can say the alphabet instead.

Skills: Group Mind, Support Your Partner, Focus, and Counting.

Teaching Tips: There should be no distinct leader, therefore each player needs to be responsible for moving the game forward.

Exercise: Skip 3's

Description: 3–12 people form a circle. Taking turns and going clockwise, players begin counting to 100. Every time a number with a 3, 6, or 9 in it pops up, instead of saying the number the player must clap his or her hands. For example, "1, 2, CLAP, 4, 5, CLAP, 7, 8, CLAP, 10, 11, 12, CLAP, 14 … ". If players mix up numbers, say a 3 number, or mess up the sequence, start over at 1.

Skills: Group Mind, Focus, Listening, Support Your Partner, and Counting.

Teaching Tips: This game can be deceptively difficult. As with any game where one member can "mess up," it is important to continue supporting your teammates rather than yelling at them or fighting with them because they said 29 instead of clapping.

Exercise: 1, 2, 3 People Walking

Description: The first of several "Viewpoints" exercises, this can be done with any number though above 20 can become a bit much – what matters is that everyone knows the exact number of people playing. Everyone simply begins silently walking around the room. The leader calls out any number between 1 and 20, for example, 4. Without speaking, four people must stop walking, while 16 continue moving. The group cannot move on until four people (and four people only) are still. Once the leader is satisfied, he or she says, "Resume walking." Taking their cue, everyone in the group starts walking again until the leader calls out a new number.

Skills: Group Mind, Making Active Choices, Giving and Taking Focus, Trusting your Partner(s), and Non-Verbal Communication.

Teaching Tips: Make sure the leader is giving numbers at a reasonable pace. Give the group time to reassemble and reset their rhythm. As the game goes on the leader can speed up the rhythm. Watch for the player that either always stops or never stops. If you notice that Logan stops every time, feel free to add in conditions like "Logan can't stop."

Exercise: Run to the Middle

Description: Another "Viewpoints" exercise where 8–12 players form a circle and begin walking (in said circle). There are several stages to the game.

Stage 1: All of the players jump at the same time. Someone watching should not be able to spot "the leader." That's because there is no leader. You are moving as a group.

Stage 2: All of the players stop moving at the same time, wait a beat, and then reverse the direction in which they're walking. Again, there is no leader.

91

Stage 3: All of the players run to the middle of the circle and form a blob, then retreat and continue walking in a circle. Again, there is no leader.

Skills: Group Mind, Awareness, Non-Verbal Communication, Focus, Letting Go of Control (if you consider yourself a leader), but also Taking Responsibility for the Group (if you consider yourself a follower).

Teaching Tips: Call out anyone who you see leading. This will happen. A lot. It takes a while for the groups to let go of the idea that someone should be leading, rather than letting things organically happen.

Exercise: Caligula

Description: The entire group. Everyone stands relatively close together and touches some part of someone else using both hands. You can fully embrace someone or simply touch them with the tip of your finger. When the coach/director/leader says "Go," everyone starts moving in any direction – *as one entity*. You can go wherever you want but you must maintain contact with the other players at all times.

Skills: Group Mind, Physicality, Support Your Partner, and "Yes, And".

Teaching Tips: It can be enticing to move very quickly, but it is often more engaging to move slowly. Don't try to plan out movements or force the movement "to make sense"; simply let the group move as an organic whole. This can get very physically tiring. Be on the lookout as the game can also be highly physical (players lifted into the air, passed around, etc.), so be sure that there is someone (coach) on the outside to help maintain safety and lend a hand if need be.

Exercises

Building upon the warm-ups, the exercises are designed to specifically work on one or more skills without the pressure of performance.

Group Mind

Exercise: Seven Things

Description: 3–12 people form a circle for this UCB staple. One member announces a category and points to another player. That player then immediately lists seven things in said category (try not to make the categories too general – colors – or too specific – nineteenth-century Senate minority leaders). If you don't know, make something up, but always start with real and/or remembered things first. The ensemble should count off and clap for each item named. When the player reaches seven, the ensemble should clap and yell, "That's seven things!" The player who just listed seven things then names a new category and points to a new player. Repeat until everyone has gone.

Skills: Getting Out of Your Head, Listening, Support Your Partner, Spontaneity, Originality, and Slow Comedy.

Teaching Tips: There are two big lessons for this game. The first is to push you past the two or three obvious and immediate things that pop into your head to exercise your improv muscle. The second is to emphasize the importance of truth and using actual memories – this is especially important for monologues and openers in long form improv. *It is always easier to remember than it is to invent.*

Exercise: Patterns

Description: 4–12 players form a circle. For the first pattern, the group picks a theme such as "Colors." One player will make eye contact with another, point to them, and say "Red." He or she will point to another player and say "Blue," and so on until each person is assigned a color, causing the last player to point to the first. This completes the pattern. Two players cannot say the same thing and each player is only pointed to once per pattern. The players should then repeat the pattern (pointing to the same person and saying the same thing) until it is firmly set. Players will then create a second pattern trying to avoid similar categories and pointing to the same people. (If I pointed at John before, I will not point at him again.) Players should try to get both patterns going at the same time. When that is successful, create a third pattern and have all three going at the same time. Mind. Blown.

Variation: Create a pattern without presetting the category. The first player will point to another, giving the group an idea. The next person will point and give that idea direction. The third will then cement the category or theme. For example:

```
1: Duck
2: Goose
3: Platypus
4-12: Would name other billed animals.
```

OR

```
1: Duck
2: Bend
3: Crouch
4-12: Would name other low to the ground posi-
       tions. See?!
```

Skills: Making Connections, Listening, Group Mind, Awareness, Attentiveness, Justification, and Adaptability.

Teaching Tips: There must be a clear distinction between patterns. Players cannot point to the same people multiple times. Feel free to take a second before answering. This isn't meant to be a free association – you are trying to create/establish/continue a pattern. Don't be afraid to take a moment… at the same time, don't sit there forever trying to think of the "right" answer. It is the group's job to make the pattern make sense. After the variation is complete, go back and talk about the thought process and development of the pattern.

Exercise: A–C Patterns

Description: Building on the Patterns game, A–C Patterns is a UCB exercise that works more with ideas and thematic connections. It can be used as an opener for a long form, or simply as a skill building tool. Similarly, 4–12 players form a circle. However, instead of sticking with a set pattern throughout, the players should skip the "B" part of the pattern. For example, let's look at the Duck-Goose-Platypus pattern from above. This pattern works to help create group mind, but in terms of idea generation it is a bit lacking. At the end of the pattern we simply have a collection of billed animals. In this version, Player 1 starts with "Duck," but rather than stick with the pattern, Player 2 should go to C. They might think "Goose," but then what does Goose lead to? "Christmas," "Migration," "Aggression," and so on. Anything really is fine, so long as it is not a straight associative response. You are looking to create ideas and themes. For instance ...

```
1: Duck
2: Christmas
3: Returning Clothes
4: Tax Deductions
5: The One Percent
```

See how we've created a lot more ideas in this version? At this point, players should recognize a pattern and go on a little riff. So, using "The One Percent" ...

```
6: Diamond Champagne
7: Diamond Champagne Engagement Ring
8: The One Percent Proposal
```

At this point we have now created what the UCB calls a premise. If this was the opener to a long form, a player could easily initiate a scene with an extravagant and elaborate proposal and everyone would recognize the reference and be able to jump right in.

After the riff, ideally the A–C pattern makes its way back to the original word or suggestion. The tendency is to continue riffing indefinitely, but you want to avoid this for several reasons. Mainly it can get tedious. But you also want to explore ideas, so getting stuck on one idea sort of defeats the purpose. So, in this case ...

```
 8: The One Percent Proposal
 9: Cutting Fat
10: Cutting Back
11: Cutting Necks
12: Duck
```

Coming back to the suggestion is called closing the loop. In an opener, you would then do another two sets of Duck-inspired A–C patterns, ultimate ending up with three separate fairly fully formed premises to play with. As a skill building exercise, it works to help players make idea and thematic connections rather than word association connections. In a scene you want to follow the scene, not simply respond to a word with an association.

Skills: Listening, Generating Ideas, Making Thematic Connections, and Group Mind.

Teaching Tips: This exercise can be complicated, so in a perfect world you would simply teach the A–C concept first since it is a bit different than traditional word association games. Then in the next rehearsal, attempt to form one loop, before going for two in the next rehearsal. Don't worry if your "B" isn't clear to everyone in the room. What's more important is that a variety of ideas are generated and a premise is found.

Exercise: Mind Meld

Description: Another UCB staple that works with any number of players forming a circle. Two players raise their hands. The rest of the group counts to three in unison. When they get to three, each player says a word. For instance, "Potato" and "Shark." Now each player must try to find the link between those words. When a player feels like he or she has the link, that player raises his or her hand. When two players have raised their hands, the group again counts to three in unison. On three, the two players each say their word. The goal is for the two players to say the same word. For instance:

```
Player 1: Potato
Player 2: Shark
```

The group now tries to link Potato and Shark.

```
Player 3: Water
Player 4: Fin
```

The group now tries to link Water and Fin.

```
Players 5 and 6: Snorkeling
```

Skills: Making Connections, Listening, Group Mind, and Spontaneity.

Teaching Tips: Do not be discouraged if it takes a few turns to make a mind meld. The more you play this game, and the more you play together as a group, the easier it will be to make connections. As with all connections, don't force them. It won't work and it'll disrupt the flow of the game. This is also a great way to come up with team names.

Exercise: Hot Spot

Description: An iO classic featuring any number of players. One player steps onto the hot spot center stage. He or she begins singing a song. It can be a real song or made up, it does not matter. As quickly as possible another player will tag him or her out and begin singing a new song. Ideally the new song will be in some way related to the original, but that isn't necessary. Players continue taking the hot spot until the game has ended.

Skills: Support Your Partner and Gagging Your Inner Critic.

Teaching Tips: A player's ability to sing does not matter. This game is all about support. The worst thing that can happen is one player left on stage for more than a few seconds. They need to feel the support of the team to do something as risky as singing.

Physicality/Object Work

Exercise: Environmental Support

Description: 6–12 players. One player steps on stage and begins an action that suggests an environment. For example, he or she might set up a beach umbrella, or push a button on an elevator, or begin scrubbing in for surgery. Once players recognize the environment, they should all fill in with complementary actions to fully build the environment. We are less concerned with building a scene, and more concerned with creating the physical environment. So you might find yourself playing inanimate objects such as waves, or elevator doors, or a scalpel.

Skills: Physicality, Group Mind, Listening, Support Your Partner, "Yes, And", and Space Work.

Teaching Tips: Don't let players over-think. Once you know they know the environment being suggested, push them into it. They will find something to do. Focus again on creating this environment as fully and realistically as possible. Don't try to be funny at all.

Exercise: Loaf of Bread

Description: 6–12 players. One at a time, players will create a space together. Each player will enter the space carrying a loaf of bread. They will then transform the bread into an object in the space (a fridge, chair, television, oven, tiny bathroom, etc.). As each new player enters the room, he or she must respect (and interact with) the previously created items/objects. Players are not allowed to describe what they are creating.

Skills: Space Work, Agreement, Attentiveness, Physicality, Non-Verbal Communication, and "Yes, And".

Teaching Tips: Make sure that players are specific. Everyone should know what he or she has created without having to say, "Look, I just made a tiny bathroom next to the oven."

Exercise: Realtor

Description: Any number of players. Each player is selling a house. He or she will take the other players on a tour, showing the best room in the house only (this can be a bedroom, bathroom, padded trampoline room with a disco ball, candy room, etc.). The player must describe and create the room before our very eyes. Everyone must be spatially aware, so if a pool is placed in the room, nobody can walk across the pool. Except Jesus. Unless you don't believe in Jesus. Which is totally okay. But probably not with Jesus.

Skills: Space Work, Agreement, Attentiveness, Physicality, and "Yes, And".

Teaching Tips: As noted, the rooms can be anything so don't feel limited to traditional rooms.

Exercise: Counter Circles

Description: Two players take the stage and begin walking in a circle (they should start on opposite ends of the stage so it looks like they are countering one another). They should not make eye contact. After a few moments, someone yells "Freeze!" The players freeze, turn their heads, and look directly at their partner. Each player should identify what he or she sees on the other person's face (fear, anxiety, joy, lust, etc.). Try not to plan a face, but let it happen naturally – often times we are unaware of all the things we are non-verbally communicating. Then let the players do a quick scene. Each player should only worry about pushing what he or she saw in the other person's face. So if I saw anger in your face, my job in this scene is to make you angry, very very angry. If you saw joy, your job would be to make me happy, very very happy.

Skills: Emotional Point of View, Agreement, Group Mind, and Listening.

Teaching Tips: Players tend to try and push their own feeling onto the other player, but really have them focus on pushing what they already see in their partner. Don't make improv harder than it needs to be – if your partner looks sad, make them really really sad. Don't try to make them feel better, make it worse. That's always a good idea in improv – make it worse.

99

Agreement

Exercise: Yes, And

Description: Any number of players, put into pairs. Player 1 begins by making a suggestion, such as, "Let's go to the store." Player 2 responds by first saying "Yes" and then adding new information, such as, "and we can pick up some milk for the party." Players then continue their conversation, agreeing and building upon each other's statements by always beginning their lines with, "Yes, and ... ".

Skills: Agreement, Support Your Partner, Active Choices, Scene Building, and Gagging Your Inner Critic.

Teaching Tips: It is corny, but make sure players always say "Yes, and" to drive home the core point of the game – agree and support. Don't worry if conversations don't make logical sense at this point, it's more important that players build off of one another.

Exercise: Yes, Let's

Description: Any number of players, in groups of up to 12. One person in the group will say, "Let's be butterflies." The other players respond with an enthusiastic, "Yes, let's!" And then the entire group pretends to be butterflies, until another player says, "Let's be zombies." Everyone responds, "Yes, let's!" And then they are zombies. And so on. There is no leader who will be calling the changes, it is up to each member of the group to call out new changes.

Skills: Agreement, Support Your Partner, Active Choices, Commitment, and Gagging Your Inner Critic.

Teaching Tips: While you might think the opposite, the player who half-heartedly takes part will actually be the one to look foolish. The more changes that are made by the group, the easier the game will become and the more willing other players will be to throw out a new idea.

Exercise: Ad Game

Description: A famous Del Close and iO exercise, this game uses any number of players, broken into groups of 4–6. The group is pretending that they are pitching a brand new product to a group of investors. They are given an everyday household item and must do the following (on the spot): 1) Find a new use for the item that isn't associated with its actual use. For example, a vacuum doesn't vacuum, instead it does your taxes). 2) Develop a slogan for the new product. For example, our new tax vacuum's slogan might be, "Suck up your refund!" 3) Develop a jingle for the product. Hint: doing anything is better than standing there staring at one another.

Skills: Agreement, "Yes, And", Support Your Partner, Listening, and Make Active Choices.

Teaching Tips: Do not let them preplan – everything must happen in the moment. For the song, as noted, doing anything such as clapping your hands, snapping your fingers, or making a generic beat will make it look like you know what you are doing and buy time to come up with lyrics.

Exercise: Crisis Situation

Description: Any number of players form two lines facing each other. Each player announces a crisis they are facing, and an unrelated item that they possess. It works best if each player tries to keep everything as unrelated as possible. The game follows the below pattern:

```
Player 1: "Help, my taco is falling apart and
     all I have is a chopstick."
Player 2: "Help, I just tore my anterior cru-
     ciate ligament and all I have is a Target
     gift card."
The players then must use his or her item to solve
     the other player's crisis. For instance …
Player 1: "Here, take my chopstick to stabilize
     your knee."
Player 2: "Thanks! Use my Target gift card as a
     shell - it's delicious!"
```

Skills: Justification, Making Connections, Listening, Support Your Partner, and Spontaneity.

Teaching Tips: As noted, try to keep things unrelated. The whole point of the game is to justify the ridiculous. When players are done with their turn they should go to the opposite line so that they don't always go first or always go second.

Initiating Scenes

Exercise: The Zero Line

Description: Any number of players form a back line. A suggestion is given and each player develops his or her "zero" line. This is essentially what he or she is going to bring to the scene. You always want to bring something with you into a scene; of course you need to be prepared to let it go instantly, but you don't want to make a habit of walking into scenes blank. The zero line can be a physical movement, a character walk, a line of dialogue, or anything else that a player might bring into a scene. At the same time, the entire back line takes a step forward (stepping into the character) and performs his or her action.

Skills: Making Active Choices, Physicality.

Teaching Tips: What a player does is not important. These scenes will never happen. The idea is to arm yourself going into a scene, or as Mick Napier says, "take care of yourself first." Keep giving new suggestions and run through a series until players get comfortable making a choice at the top of a scene.

102

Exercise: Initiations

Description: Any number of players broken into two lines. An initiation (sometimes called a declaration or bid line) is the first line of a scene and should establish three things: Relationship, Location, and Emotional Point Of View. For instance, the line "Mom, get out of my room!" is an excellent initiation because it describes who you are, where you are, and how you feel about the other person, in this case your mother.

Variations:

- Physical Initiation: starting the scene with a non-verbal action.
- Name Initiation: starting the scene by only saying the other character's name, with feeling or intent.
- Emotional POV Initiation: starting the scene by declaring a strong emotional point of view directly connected to the other person in the scene.
- Second Line: the response to the Initiation. Must agree with and add new information to the scene. Remember, this is the second line of a scene, not the best comeback.

Skills: Scene Building, Agreement, Active Choices, Support Your Partner, Listening, Character Development, and Emotional Investment.

Teaching Tips: The Initiation is not a joke. The second line is not a comeback. The point of this exercise is to lay the foundation for starting successful scenes. It is also common for players to force rather than discover. For instance: "Beth, my sister, please put the instant mashed potatoes into our shopping cart here at the grocery store." Feels forced, right? Instead, discover it or let it be more natural: "Jenny, put the potatoes in the cart." We get a lot more from the second line because it is natural (and it also tells us where we are and who is in the scene).

Exercise: Goalie

Description: 6–12 players. One player is the goalie. The other players, in rapid succession, deliver bid lines to the goalie who must then reply with a second line to each. The goalie may rotate throughout the game.

Skills: Attentiveness, Spontaneity, Listening, Being Present, Character Building, Scene Building, and Agreement.

Teaching Tips: As with Bid Lines, the second line is not a comeback, it is a building block.

Exercise: Three-Line Scenes

Description: Any number of players broken into two lines. Building off of Bid Line and Goalie, players will perform the first three lines of a scene. This is not necessarily a scene that happens within three lines, but the first three lines of a theoretically larger scene.

One line will begin the scene with a non-verbal action, while the other has the responsibility of verbally initiating in reaction to the first player. When the scene is complete, after the three lines are said, the other players will say "3, 2, 1!" and clap. This will be the cue for the next actors to take the stage and begin their scene. After the players are finished, they will switch lines.

Variations: It can be helpful to stop after three lines and then discuss everything you know about the characters, the setting, and the situation. Then talk about what might happen in the scene, where you might take a particular character … in short, what this scene is going to be about. It's also fun to have a leader randomly pick scenes to continue beyond three lines.

Skills: Attentiveness, Spontaneity, Listening, Being Present, Character Building, Scene Building, and Agreement.

Teaching Tips: Remember strong initiations, and remember this is not a scene in three lines. Relationship, location, and emotional point of view must be present and built off of.

Exercise: Four-Line Scenes

Description: Any number of players, broken into pairs. Much like Bid Lines, this exercise attempts to overtly define the relationship, location, and emotional point of view for a scene. The exercise goes as follows:

```
Player 1: I am _____ (who). I am
          _____ (doing some activity).
Player 2: I am _____ (who). We are
          _____ (where).
Player 1: I feel _____ (about you/this
          situation).
Player 2: I feel _____ (about you/this
          situation).
```

Players can then continue the scene using this information, while hopefully driving home the importance of establishing the relationship, location, and point of view.

Skills: Scene Building, Listening, Being Present, Character Building, and Agreement.

Teaching Tips: This exercise can make the dialogue feel unnatural … and that's because it is unnatural. The point is to emphasize the importance of getting that information out as soon as possible.

Exercise: Heat and Weight

Description: Heat and Weight is at the core of TJ & Dave's improv philosophy, so let's explain it a bit before we get to the exercise. The "weight" is the way a line is delivered. Scenes are generally either light or heavy. If my cat died last night there is a different weight to the line "We're out of Cheerios" than if we had amazing sex last night. The key to "weight" is to respond to the "weight" your partner is giving you, not the information. If your partner is happy or sad, you are responding to his or her happiness or sadness, not the actual information he or she gave you. I don't care about Cheerios; I care about the "weight" of what's happening between these two people. You should be able to strip away the words or completely change the dialogue without losing the relationship because the weight is what's important. The "heat" is the nature of the relationship, which goes much deeper than the title of the relationship (mother-son). Some relationships are hot and some are cold (note that hot doesn't only mean lust). There's usually a corollary between heat and weight.

Players break into pairs. Multiple pairs can go at the same time, or you can call each pair to the stage. Step 1: Player A should make a conscious decision about a character, with a specific occupation, status, age, emotional point of view, etc., and/or a specific situation that would elicit an emotional response ("You're my roommate and I just caught you cheating with my girlfriend."). The more specific the better. Player A then strikes a physical pose that communicates as much as possible about the character. Player B then takes a moment to examine Player A, and then tells Player A what he or she sees. Player A then tells Player B what his or her original intention was. Players can discuss further before switching roles. Step 2: Both players should strike a pose as in Step 1. They should take each other in without breaking their poses. Based on the information they feel they are receiving, they can then begin a scene.

Skills: Physicality, Emotional Point of View, Take Care of Yourself, and Listening.

Teaching Tips: Listening isn't just about listening to words; it's also about listening to what your partner is telling you physically. The more specific you can be – both as Player A and B – the better. Bringing a strong physicality and point of view helps bring heat and weight to the scene. Don't worry about getting every detail right – worry about getting the heat and weight correct. You should be able to read the tone and relationship from just looking at one another. This is a good exercise to emphasize "Why you two? Why now?"

Exercise: Silent Connection

Description: Players break into pairs. Multiple pairs can go at the same time, or you can call each pair to the stage. Two players stand across from each other. Much like Heat and Weight, the goal is to communicate character, connect with your scene partner, and realize what is already between you and your scene partner without having to invent. In this exercise everything is done without miming, striking a pose, or speaking. Once again Player A should make a conscious choice about his or her character: what's the relationship, what do you want, what's the situation, etc. Player B simply receives the information and then tells Player A what he or she got from the other person's energy and body language.

Skills: Connecting with your Scene Partner (Group Mind), Listening, and Awareness.

Teaching Tips: Be real and honest. Your initial impulse is to either pantomime or over-exaggerate physically. If you are about to tell your boyfriend that you love him for the first time, think about the type of energy you'd be radiating, think about how you'd hold your body – think about how you'd look at him. Then do it. If you are Player A, don't change your intentions based on Player B's response just to be "right." Obviously if you were in a scene you would "Yes, And," but in this exercise the goal is to establish a connection with your scene partner and recognize what is already between you without having to invent.

106

Building Scenes

Exercise: A–B

Description: Any number of players in pairs. This classic Keith Johnstone exercise is about free association and reincorporation. Player A is given thirty seconds in which they free-associate a number of statements. These statements should not be related to one another. Player B must then connect these free associations into a story, incorporating everything that Player A had stated.

Example:

Player A: A red ball. A deserted ocean. A man sitting next to an air conditioner. Wolves around a fire, roasting marshmallows.

Player B: It's the end of a very hot summer. A man abandons his camping trip after his girlfriend breaks up with him and now sits alone sobbing beneath his air conditioner. He left everything behind that reminds him of her, including her favorite treat: marshmallows. A pack of wolves has been unable to hunt due to the heat, and stumbles upon the marshmallows. They begin roasting them. One of the wolves accidently kicks a red ball into the fire, sparking a gigantic forest fire. The wolves flee, and the once mighty forest resembles a deserted ocean.

Skills: Free Association, Reincorporation, Story Telling, Scene Building, Listening, Justification, Trust, and Spontaneity.

Teaching Tips: Make sure Player A keeps his/her ideas far apart, allowing Player B the freedom to connect them. All information should be used in the scene; there is no such thing as a throwaway.

Exercise: Color/Advance

Description: Any number of players in pairs. This exercise focuses on storytelling by adding color and/or advancing the plot. This is also a good exercise to help build scene-painting skills. One improviser is the storyteller, the other is the CA. The storyteller begins telling a story. At any point the CA can give one of two commands: 1) more color; 2) advance the plot. After a set amount of time (usually between two and five minutes) the improvisers switch roles.

Example:

```
Storyteller: I was riding the bus home from work
     last night—
CA: More color on the bus.
```

Storyteller: It's the 143 that runs north and south down State Street. The same people ride it every day, and it has this overwhelming feeling of sadness. Like the saddest people in the world ride this bus. The driver's name is Owen—

CA: More color on Owen.

Storyteller: Owen is in his mid-40s. He's been divorced four times - if a new person ever gets on the bus he tells them all about his first ex-wife. Second ride they get the second and so on until they are a regular. His fourth ex-wife actually gets on at 23rd everyday.

CA: Advance (the plot)!

Storyteller: So I'm riding home last night and I'm always the last one to get off. Owen stops the bus a block early and he just starts sobbing.

CA: Color.

Storyteller: These are the tears of a man that hasn't cried in 30 years. They are working to get out of him. It's like he doesn't know how to cry. He's making this awful sound that he's simultaneously trying to suppress and express.

CA: Advance.

Storyteller: I don't say anything. I get up to get off the bus, figuring he thought he was alone. I start opening the door manually and I feel this arm wrap around me. Owen's hugging me. I don't know what to do here. I've never been hugged by a bus driver.

CA: Color.

Storyteller: I should mention that I hate being touched. I'm totally uncomfortable with touching. It just grosses me out.

CA: Advance!

Storyteller: So he's just got this one arm around me. Tight. He's got a really strong grip

108

```
on me. I try to wiggle free but it's not
working. He finally stops crying and lets
go and I don't know what came over me, but
I turn around and give him this giant hug.
```

Skills: Storytelling, Building a Scene, Scene Painting, Listening, "Yes, And", and Support Your Partner.

Teaching Tips: Your goal as the CA is to "edit" the story. It is very easy to get too caught up in plot and/or color. Your whole job is to keep the momentum moving forward. Sometimes that is best done with plot and sometimes it is done with color. Really focus on making the story specific – if you are having trouble, try telling a fairy tale so that the plot is already taken care of and you just need to find the proper places to add more color to the story. Remember that the plot is supposed to be fun, so don't get too caught up in plot details – that's what the color is for! And vice-versa; all the color in the world ultimately doesn't work if there isn't any sort of plot to ground it.

Exercise: Repetition

Description: Players split into pairs. Yes, this is the Meisner exercise. Two players face one another with a sense of ease and place their attention on each other. You want to make a connection with each other, and call attention to the other's behavior. Without thinking about it, one player names the behavior they see in the other. The players then repeat this information. For instance:

```
Player 1: You're mad.
Player 2: I'm mad.
Player 1: You're mad.
Player 2: I'm mad.
```

The players should react in the moment. They shouldn't say the lines rote, rather they should let what is happening affect them. At any point, when the moment is right, either player can say something new. So continuing off of the above:

```
Player 1: I'm sorry.
Player 2: You're sorry?
Player 1: I'm sorry.
Player 2: You're sorry.
```

```
Player 1: I said I was sorry.
Player 2: You said you were sorry.
```

And so on. Make sure to keep your attention on the other person, and stay in the moment. Keep everything real and immediate, don't say things that the other person isn't doing or that aren't true.

Skills: Spontaneity, Character Point of View, Emotional Point of View, and Reaction.

Teaching Tips: Players will struggle at first and feel awkward. That's good. Encourage them to feel that and react to it rather than try to ignore it. Don't edit out mistakes and don't censor yourself. Let it be messy, let it be real, let it be in the moment.

Exercise: That's Important to Me

Description: Two players. You are building a scene by using the information given to you by your partner and then literally stating why it is important to you. For instance:

110

```
A: You're arm looks pretty bad.
B: My arm looks pretty bad, and that's important
   to me because I'm scared.
A: You're scared, and that's important to me
   because I'm your father and I want to pro-
   tect you.
B: You want to protect me, and that's important
   to me because I don't want to let you down.
A: You don't want to let me down, and that's
   important to me because I don't want you to
   feel like you ever have to prove something
   to me.
```

And so on ...

Skills: Listening, Reincorporation, Scene Building, Emotional Point of View, Character Point of View, and Spontaneity.

Teaching Tips: This will feel awkward at first, but if you allow what the other person is saying to truly land, you will easily be able to express why it is important to you. Don't make it a jokey thing – try your best to be honest. In fact, often you will build quite serious scenes. That's great! Eventually you should get to the point where you are answering the "why it's important to me" without having to be overt about it. This exercise is great for getting scene partners to focus on each other and how they relate to one another instead of the circumstance.

Exercise: Solo Character Switches

Description: Any number of players can go at the same time, but this Mick Napier game is a solitary exercise. A player begins a character monologue. It can be helpful to give players a prompt, or they can just start. After a set time (usually no more than 30 seconds) the leader yells "Switch!" At this point the player begins a completely new character monologue. Ideally the new monologue is not in response to or conversation with the first, but a completely new situation. This continues until the leader feels the game is over or everyone passes out.

Skills: Character Development, Character Point of View, Emotional Point of View, Spontaneity, and Gagging Your Inner Critic.

Teaching Tips: If players are struggling, remind them that playing opposites is an easy way to differentiate/create new characters (high status to low status, exuberant to depressed, apathetic to overly engaged).

111

Exercise: One Actor, Two Characters

Description: Any number of players, but again, this Napier game is a solitary exercise. In this exercise the player is playing both characters in the scene, bouncing back and forth between them.

Skills: Character Development, Character Point of View, Emotional Point of View, Spontaneity, and Gagging Your Inner Critic.

Teaching Tips: If players are struggling, remind them that playing opposites is an easy way to differentiate/create new characters (high status to low status, exuberant to depressed, apathetic to overly engaged).

Exercise: Three-Way Conversation

Description: Any number of players split into groups of three. The players should form a triangle and designate one player as the "middle." The player in the middle is holding an independent conversation with each of the other two players. The other two players, however, are only having a conversation with the player in the middle and should completely disregard the other outside player. They should both be speaking to the player in the middle simultaneously (don't take turns). The player in the middle must negotiate between the two conversations (not necessarily joining them together), but make each player feel like he or she is receiving full attention.

Skills: Listening, Spontaneity, and Support Your Partner.

Teaching Tips: Don't let the outside players be too nice. Don't let them take turns with one another. If you were having a conversation with someone who wasn't giving you his or her undivided attention, you'd be mad. Feel free to rotate positions so each player is in the middle.

Exercise: Give and Take

Description: A variant of iO's Cocktail Party, this exercise uses groups of six players, who are then divided into three sets of pairs. Each pair will be holding an independent conversation. Initially a conductor will point to each pair, signifying when they are to speak. As the game progresses, the conductor fades out and the pairs become responsible for shifting focus. The pairs can begin to make thematic connections, but tying everything together into one story is not the focus of the game. Instead, organically sharing focus is the main goal.

Skills: Sharing Focus, Agreement, Scene Building, Character Development, Listening, Active Choices, and Editing.

Teaching Tips: Give enough time initially so that each pair can set up a solid scene. If the characters don't want anything it will be more difficult to tell when to cut to or away from the scene.

Exercise: Master–Servant

Description: As with most status exercises, this is a Johnstone classic. Any number of players, but broken up into pairs. One player is the Master while the other is the Servant. The Master demands various things/items/actions, and it is the Servant's job to justify and perform the actions. For example:

```
Master: "Bring me a chair."
Servant: "Of course, for you must be tired after
    winning so many wars."
Master: "Thank you. But you forgot my tiny
    spatula."
Servant: "How silly of me. How else will you
    flip your tiny 'spoils of war' burgers?"
```

```
Master:  "Delicious.  Could  you  please  fetch
    me   my   scratch   and   sniff   stickers?"
    Servant:  "I  know  how  they  help  relax  you
    before  seeing  the  Queen."
```

Skills: Justification, Agreement, Support Your Partner, Listening, and Being Present.

Teaching Tips: It is actually much more difficult (for some) to be the Master since they are constantly providing information – and can be a good example of the difficulty of having a passive partner who only reacts to the information you are providing. Don't forget to develop a scene by creating a world with characters with specific needs, rather than just listing demands – this will make the game easier to play. That means *both* the Master and Servant should work to justify and heighten together.

Exercise: Status Party

Description: Any number of players, broken into groups of 8–12. The players number off 1 to X, with 1 being the lowest status. The group develops a social situation that these people are at, such as a cocktail party, barbeque, or birthday party. The group has three minutes to plan their scenario, and then must act and react to each other according to their status. After a few minutes the other players then try to determine the status of the partygoers.

Skills: Status, Character Development, Agreement, and Listening.

Teaching Tips: Status can be conveyed in a number of ways so the high-status person doesn't always have to be an asshole. Make sure that players are listening to one another and not creating three or four independent scenes within the larger scene.

Exercise: Status Swap

Description: Any number of players, but broken up into pairs. Similar to Master–Servant, at the beginning of the scene there should be a clear status hierarchy (this can be given to the players or it can develop organically). Player 1 should have the high status, while Player 2 is low status. At some point in the scene Player 2 must take the status from Player 1. If you are so bold, Player 1 can then attempt to retake the status from Player 2.

Skills: Status, Justification, Agreement, Character Development, Support Your Partner, Scene Building, and Listening.

Teaching Tips: Don't rush the swap. A typical scene will start with one status, have a swap in the middle, and end with a final status battle. If you develop a scene with strong character wants, the swap will most likely happen organically.

Exercise: Crutch Dialogue

Description: One of Michael Gellman's best exercises that can use any number of players, broken into pairs. Players are given a series of vague/meaningless lines such as, "How are you?" "Where is it?" "Nice day today." "Great party." etc. The players then develop a scene using the crutch dialogue, but giving the lines meaning through character, objectives, location, physicality, and emotional point of view.

Skills: Scene Building, Character Development, Agreement, Support Your Partner, Emotional Point of View, and Listening.

Teaching Tips: The intent behind what you say is more important than what you say. Really challenge players to create a fully developed scene rather than letting them simply run through the lines and then say, "Oh, we were brothers." Remember, the *how* is more important than the *what* (this goes for object work too).

Exercise: Back-To-Back Chairs

Description: Any number of players, split into groups of three. Two players sit in chairs that are placed back to back. The third player will act as a sort of coach/inner monologue for both players. The players can be given a relationship, location, or any other prompt (or no prompt at all). Before either player speaks, the coach will ask questions about the given circumstances. For instance, the players are told that they are sisters. The coach might ask them about their relationship, who is older, who has a better relationship with their parents, and what each one wants from the other in this interaction. None of these questions are to be verbally answered by the players, but should instead act as a moment to reflect and set up what is to come. Player 1 then starts with a bid line. From this point forward, neither player can speak until the coach says "Line." During the down time between lines, the coach can ask questions or direct the next line (e.g. "Take the status." "Tell her what you want right now."). The idea is to slow down a scene so that players can really focus on the meaning and power of their lines, and really listen and react to their partner's lines.

Skills: Scene Building, Listening, Character Development, Agreement, Support Your Partner, Make Active Choices, Being Present, and Spontaneity/Slow Comedy.

Teaching Tips: Keep the pace slow. Really allow players the time to think about what has just been said and how they will respond. The coach isn't trying to dictate what happens in the scene – he or she is trying to open possibilities.

Exercise: Freeze

Description: 3–16 players. Two players take the stage and the others form a semi-circle behind them. The two players are given a physical position and begin a scene. At any point a player on the back line can yell, "FREEZE!", at which point the actors freeze, and he or she assumes the physical position of one of the actors (more than one actor can be replaced). They then start a completely new scene, incorporating (and justifying) their positions. This process continues until the game has ended, which can be at any point you'd like.

Variations:

Dirty Freeze – Any player can yell freeze and then call another player into the scene rather than going in themselves.

Blind Freeze – The players not on stage either have their eyes closed or backs to the action so that when "Freeze" is called they must jump into the action without preplanning.

Skills: Justification, Spontaneity, Support Your Partner, Physicality, and Active Choices.

Teaching Tips: Make sure actors commit to their "freeze" positions and incorporate them into the scene. Keep the pace up, but also watch for the game becoming a series of one-line jokes. Feel free to call in reluctant players, or to call out overzealous players who are in every other scene.

Exercise: I Remember…

Description: 2 players. They get a topic from the audience or coach. The idea is to start with a series of personal memories in a conversational format. You are simply talking to the other person, not trying to do a scene, make it funny, or find "the game." For the first few lines, each player should start with, "I remember… " As the conversation progresses, players should begin to build off of one another (just like a scene) and eventually the players should be having a

115

scenic-style conversation. Let everything organically emerge from real and personal experiences. For example, the suggestion is "beach":

```
Player 1: I remember going to the beach as a
          kid. We only lived about 20 minutes from
          the beach, but we hardly ever went. So when
          we did go it was a really big deal.
Player 2: I remember the first time I went into
          the ocean. I'm from the Midwest so when I
          got the saltwater in my mouth it was like
          this total paradigm shift for me.
Player 1: I remember the first time a girl asked
          me out. I had a really 1950s mentality as
          a nine year old. This real sense of honor.
          So when a girl asked me out, I was totally
          floored.
Player 2: Gender roles are really silly if you
          think about them.
Player 1: Right? Like we are inherently bred as
          men to like blue and despise pink.
Player 2: I love pink.
Player 1: I know. And for a long time I felt
          really bad about it.
```

As you can see, the scene organically emerges from the personal experiences/memories.

Skills: Scene Building, Agreement, "Yes, And", Listening, and Truth in Comedy.

Teaching Tips: A lot of players resist letting their guard down and try to be funny right away. That kills the scene. So let them do it, and then make sure they realize what killed the scene was "trying" to be funny. The exercise is all about grounding your scene work in reality. Every scene, no matter how wacky it may become, needs a base reality. This exercise can also help improvisers stuck in their heads because everyone has memories they can share.

Short Form Improv Games

Short form improv is a very popular and stylized form of improvisation. Audiences tend to be more familiar with it than long form. And lots of college groups perform short form. As noted in the Introduction, short form improv is game based. Each game usually has a specific gimmick or handle that makes the game work (and is the structural source of comedy). Games and characters usually live and die with a particular game, though more and more groups are bringing long form elements into short form games and connecting things together.

Short form games can also be used as exercises. Many short form games were originally Spolin exercises, so feel free to use any of these games to work on a particular skill even if you never intend to perform short form or a particular game in front of an audience.

This section catalogues a number of short form games, but by no means is exhaustive. There are many more games to play – you can even create your own!

- Guessing Games
  - Party Quirks
  - Dead Guy
  - Dating Game
  - Press Conference
  - Good Cop, Bad Cop
  - Themed Restaurant
  - Late to Class
  - Customer Return

- Scenic Games
  - First Line – Last Line
  - Last Letter – First Letter
  - Alphabet Game
  - Four Square
  - Emotional Quadrants
  - Entrances and Exits
  - Trigger Word
  - Mannequins
  - Scene Genre
  - Ding
  - Director's Cut
  - Evil Twin
  - Siamese Twin
  - Dual Situations
  - Dual Speak
  - Pyramid Freeze Tag
  - Sit, Stand, Lie Down
  - Dubbing
  - Slips of Paper
  - Actor's Nightmare
  - He Said, She Said

118

- Group Games
  - Beastie Boys
  - Photo Album
  - Game-O-Matic
  - Expert
- Energy Games
  - Survivor
  - Sportscasters
  - Superheroes
  - Half-Life
  - Taxi
  - Grand Theft Auto
- Narrative Games
  - Fortunately/Unfortunately
  - One-Word Story
  - Conducted Story
  - Pen Name
  - Documentary
  - Poet's Corner
  - Did You Say?
- Ask the Audience Games
  - Buddha
  - Good, Bad, Ugly
  - Gibberish Translator
  - Audience Text
- One-Liner Games
  - World's Worst
  - 185
  - I Like My …

119

Guessing Games

Game: Party Quirks

Description: 4 players. One player is selected (either beforehand or by the audience) to host the party, and leaves the room. The other three players are all guests at the party, and have an unusual quirk that the host must guess (walks on toes, starts sentences with the letter s, is a melting snowman, etc.). The host establishes the scene, and then at thirty-second intervals the guests enter the party. Guests are free to speak to one another as well as the host. When the host guesses a quirk, that player must justify his or her exit. The game ends when the host successfully guesses all three quirks.

Skills: Character Development, Physicality, Listening, Support Your Partner, and Spontaneity.

Teaching Tips: As with all short form games, do not solely rely on the gimmick. Create relationships and an environment that will actually make the game easier to play. Try to weave your questions within dialogue rather than bluntly stating the quirk. If the host has no idea, any player can help.

Game: Dead Guy

Description: 4 players and an emcee. Each of the four detectives can only communicate non-verbally. One detective stays and the other three leave the room. The emcee solicits the following from the audience: Who has died? Where did they die? And how did they die? The first detective therefore knows exactly what happened. One by one each detective enters the room. The previous detective will then non-verbally convey what happened. When a detective thinks he or she knows a particular element, he or she touches his or her nose to move onto the next clue. Once they think they know all three, the next detective enters, and so on. So, Detective 1 "tells" Detective 2. Detective 2 "tells" Detective 3. Detective 3 "tells" Detective 4. After all four detectives have gone, the emcee lines them up and asks them in reverse order what happened.

Skills: Non-Verbal Communication, Physicality, Attentiveness, Spontaneity, and Support Your Partner.

Teaching Tips: It is more fun to watch and more challenging to play if each detective finds a new way to convey the information, rather than simply repeating what was given to them. If a detective has no idea what something is, it is best to keep the game moving, so touch your nose and do your best. The humor comes from things being lost in translation.

Game: Dating Game

Description: 5 players. One player is the Contestant, one is the Host, and three are the Bachelor/Bachelorettes. The Contestant leaves the room. Each Bachelor/Bachelorette is given a quirk, persona, etc. The

Contestant then tries to figure out the quirks/personas by asking dating-related questions. Typically, the Contestant will ask one or two general questions that each player may answer, and then one or two specific questions for individual Bachelor/Bachelorettes. The players should incorporate their quirks/personas into their answers as organically as possible. The Host both moves the game along and can help by throwing in a clue or two along the way. At the end of the game the Contestant begins by saying who he or she does not want to date (and in the process naming who they are – "I don't think I'll go with Bachelor #1. I'm just not into ferrets with cars.") The Contestant then picks the winner.

Skills: Character Development, Physicality, Attentiveness, Spontaneity, and Support Your Partner.

Teaching Tips: The Host must keep the game moving, and should remember that he or she knows the quirks/personas so can always help out. Balance the line of giving enough information without totally giving your quirk away at the top.

Game: Press Conference

Description: 1 player and a host. The player leaves the room. The host asks the audience for a well-known person, who the player unknowingly embodies. The player returns, and the audience begin asking questions of the player. The host should encourage beginning with general questions before asking person-specific questions, which should continue until the player figures out who they are and is able to end the press conference as said person.

Skills: Listening, Spontaneity, Attentiveness, Being Present in the Moment, and Character Development.

Teaching Tips: It's always more fun to make bold claims, rather than vague statements. If you don't know who you are and the clues aren't helping you, continue to make big statements, and if it comes down to it, simply storm off.

Game: Good Cop, Bad Cop

Description: 3 players. One player is the criminal, one is the good cop, and one is the bad cop. The criminal leaves the room. The audience tells the cops the following: What the crime was, what he or she did it with, and who he or she did it with (shaved your legs, with a cactus, with Harry Potter). The cops then interrogate the criminal, trying to get them to confess. Both the good and the bad cop should drop hints and clues as they interrogate the criminal. The good cop and bad cop can switch personas if they so choose.

Skills: Listening, Attentiveness, Spontaneity, and Support Your Partner.

Teaching Tips: Give clues for one section at a time. Mixing clues will confuse the criminal. As with all guessing games, part of the enjoyment is that the audience knows something that a player does not. So don't panic if you can't figure things out. If all else fails, the cops can simply ask, "Did you shave your legs with a cactus, and have Harry Potter help you?" Always say yes to this question.

Game: Themed Restaurant

Description: 3 players – a waiter, a date, and our hero. The hero leaves the room. The audience is asked for a specific theme for the restaurant. The hero returns and sits down at a table with his or her date. The waiter enters and begins a normal waiter-customer transaction, incorporating some aspect of the theme. This continues until the hero can guess the theme.

Skills: Listening, Attentiveness, Spontaneity, Character Development, and Support Your Partner.

Teaching Tips: As with all guessing games, if you know the answer quickly, still play the game for a bit rather than instantly blurting out the answer. The waiter can also bring his or her manager to the table if more help is needed.

Game: Late to Class

Description: 5 players – a teacher, the late student, and three other students. The late student leaves the room. The audience is then asked: Why is the student late? What happened on the way to school? And how did the student finally get there? When the late student arrives, the teacher pulls him or her aside. While the teacher's back is to the other students, they begin pantomiming each scenario, one at a time. If the teacher looks back at the other students, they must freeze and justify their positions. The game ends when the late student correctly guesses.

Skills: Non-Verbal Communication, Physicality, Attentiveness, Spontaneity, and Support Your Partner.

Teaching Tips: Only give clues for one segment at a time. When the student has guessed correctly, the audience should applaud, signifying that it is okay to move on to the next section. If one pantomime or motion is not clearly conveying the message, the players must figure out a new way to relay the message rather than simply repeating the old unhelpful motion again and again.

Game: Customer Return

Description: 3 players. One player leaves the room. He or she is returning a product to a store. The audience provides said product/item. One player is the cashier, and the third is the store manager who is called over if the cashier needs additional assistance relaying information to the customer. The players act out a normal store return, where the cashier drops hints and clues to the customer about what the item actually is.

Skills: Listening, Attentiveness, Spontaneity, and Support Your Partner.

Teaching Tips: As with all guessing games, try not to give it away in the beginning, and for the guesser make big bold statements.

Scenic Games

Game: First Line – Last Line

Description: 2 players, though it can be played with more. The audience gives the players the first line of dialogue in the scene, and the last line of dialogue in the scene. The players then create a scene that links the beginning and end.

Skills: Scene Building, Agreement, Making Active Choices, Connections, and Support Your Partner.

Teaching Tips: When soliciting lines, make sure that they have no obvious connection – that will actually make it easier for the players. This is as close to a "blank scene" as there is in short form, so above all else you must create a good solid scene because there isn't really a gimmick to fall back on.

Game: Last Letter – First Letter

Description: 2 players, though it can be played with more. In this game each line of dialogue must begin with the last letter of the last word spoken by the previous player. For example:

```
Player 1: "Pass me the mustard."
Player 2: "Don't you ask me for mustard, Dan.
    Not after what you've done."
```

> Player 1: "*Everybody* was doing it, Evelyn. Cut
> me a break. You did it too!"
> Player 2: "*Oh*, so now it's my fault?"
> Player 1: "*Totally.*"
> Player 2: "*You're* right. Please forgive me."

Skills: Listening, Agreement, Scene Building, Focus, Attentiveness, and Support Your Partner.

Teaching Tips: As with all short form games, don't rely on the gimmick, exploit the gimmick. You still need to construct a relationship between two specific people that want something from one another. The gimmick is then layered onto that relationship. And as always, have fun – throw in some pauses to keep your partner on their toes. Don't feel burdened by the gimmick – *use* the gimmick.

Game: Alphabet Game

Description: 2 players, though it can be played with more. Similar to Last Letter – First Letter, each line of dialogue in this game starts with the next letter of the alphabet. Players are given a letter to start and must make their way through the alphabet at least once. For example, the starting letter is W:

> Player 1: "*William*, I need you to break up with me."
> Player 2: "*Xavier*, I'll only do it if you give
> me your Russian teapot."
> Player 1: "*You* know my mother gave that to me
> for my birthday."
> Player 2: "*Zoo* trips. Not everything is about
> your mother and the zoo."
> Player 1: "*Absolutely* this is about my mother
> and the zoo. And you know it."
> Player 2: "*Because* I set up the trip. She bought
> that teapot for me."

Skills: Listening, Agreement, Scene Building, Focus, and Support Your Partner.

Teaching Tips: Again, don't rely on the gimmick. Create a relationship and explore the relationship by using the gimmick.

Game: Four Square

Description: 4 players, with a fifth to rotate the players (this can also be the host). The players form a square with two players facing the audience, and two players behind them. Generally the fifth player or host will solicit a prompt **for each pair** before beginning the game. Whichever set of two is in front facing the audience is the "live" set, and their scene is active. For the below example, Players A and B would be the "live" scene:

C   D (upstage)
A   B (downstage)

Each player will be in two separate unrelated scenes during the game, playing two totally different and unconnected characters. The fifth player or host will call to rotate the players between scenes. A "Shift Right" would then look like this, with Players B and D in the "live" scene:

A   C
B   D

The fifth player or host can call out a Shift Right, Shift Left, or he or she can do a double Shift Right or Left by simply saying Shift Right (or Left) twice in a row. From the previous position, a "Shift Right Shift Right" would look like this, with Players C and A in the "live" scene:

D   B
C   A

Skills: Character Development, Bid Lines, Scene Building, Multiple Scenes (prep for connections), Support Your Partner, Editing, and Listening.

Teaching Tips: Make big and bold choices to distinguish your characters. Play opposites – different status, emotional points of view, wants, etc. For the fifth player or host, let each scene establish itself briefly before jumping too much between scenes. The fifth player or host is vital to the success of the game, so do not overlook the importance of properly editing each scene.

Game: Emotional Quadrants

Description: 2 players, though it can be played with more. The stage is broken into four imaginary quadrants. Each quadrant is assigned an emotion by the audience (fear, love, regret, apprehension, etc.). Player 1 is the control player and is unaffected by the audience-assigned emotions (he or she can still have emotions, they simply aren't tied to a quadrant of the stage). Player 2 must match his or her emotion to the quadrant they are in. It is up to both players to justify the emotional switches.

Variation: Instead of breaking the stage into quadrants, place several props on the stage and endow each with an emotion. When a player is holding a prop, he or she must use its assigned emotion (it's often fun to hold two objects at the same time and use both emotions).

Skills: Justification, Emotional Point of View, Listening, Agreement, Making Active Choices, and Support Your Partner.

Teaching Tips: As always, don't rely on the gimmick. Create an actual scene between two characters that each want something and let the emotions heighten those wants. It is also helpful to place an object or clearly define each quadrant so that Player 2 (or 1) has a logical reason to move from quadrant to quadrant.

Game: Entrances and Exits

Description: 4 players. The audience gives each player a trigger word (duck, sister, hamburger, etc.). Whenever a trigger word is said in the course of the scene, the corresponding player must either enter the scene if he or she is offstage, or exit the scene if he or she is currently on stage. Players *must justify* why they are entering or exiting the scene.

Skills: Listening, Justification, Spontaneity, Agreement, Support Your Partner, and Scene Building.

Teaching Tips: Do not simply just rattle off trigger words. Instead, create a scene and use the trigger words to heighten the situation. Always remember that the players are in control of who is on stage (and off) at all times. That is a powerful tool. Also remember that you can call yourself offstage by saying your own word.

Game: Trigger Word

Description: 3 players. As with Entrances and Exits, each player is given a trigger word. In this game, whenever a player's word is said

126

he or she must perform a physical bit, which is given to each player by the audience before the game begins. Players must justify their bits rather than just randomly performing them.

Skills: Listening, Justification, Spontaneity, Agreement, Support Your Partner, and Scene Building.

Teaching Tips: Do not simply rattle off trigger words. Instead, create a scene and use the trigger words to heighten the situation. Do your best to incorporate your physical bit – justify!

Game: Mannequins

Descriptions: 2–4 players (or two players and two audience volunteers). Two players are mannequins, and are unable to move by themselves. The other two players must move the mannequins throughout the game. The mannequins are the only players that speak, and must justify every movement.

Skills: Scene Development, Justification, Physicality, Agreement, Support Your Partner, and Spontaneity.

Teaching Tips: Allow time for the mannequins to justify their positions before moving them again. Step back and give them a moment to incorporate the physical changes into the scene. Mannequins can also request or imply movements ("I've got to get something from the fridge.").

127

Game: Scene Genre

Description: 2–5 players. Players perform a scene with great relationships, high stakes, and strong character wants/emotions. The audience then gives the players a different genre and the players repeat the original scene in said genre (Western, Action, Romance, etc.). Typically the originally scene is repeated in three different genres.

Skills: Scene Development, Character Development, Agreement, Support Your Partner, and Spontaneity.

Teaching Tips: The original scene is the base for the game, so really focus on doing a quality scene. Make bold choices with the given genres, especially if you have no idea what a particular genre should be like. Don't feel tied to the original scene verbatim. You are recreating the essence so feel free to give yourself some artistic license.

Game: Ding

Description: 3 players. Two players are doing a scene. At any point in the scene the third player can say, "Ding!" With each "Ding!" the last line said must be changed. For example:

```
Player 1: "Let's go to the park."
Player 3: "Ding!"
Player 1: "Let's go to the mall."
Player 3: "Ding!"
Player 1: "I have syphilis."
```

The end of the game is up to Player 3.

Variations: Some folks call this game "New Choice" or "Shoulda Said." Instead of saying "Ding" you say "New Choice" or "Shoulda Said." These two options give you a little more freedom because you can be a bit more specific. For instance, "New Emotion," or "New Reaction."

Skills: Scene Development, Spontaneity, Adaptability, Gagging Your Inner Critic, Support Your Partner, and Listening.

Teaching Tips: As with Scene Genre, the game depends on a solid base scene. The timing of the "Dings" is what makes the game work. Look for times to heighten the scene, raise the stakes, etc. Too much dinging causes confusion, while not enough leaves the scene lacking variety and misses the crux of the game.

Game: Director's Cut

Description: 3–5 players. One player is designated the Director and begins by soliciting various emotions, nouns, etc. from the audience, which he or she quickly jots down. The other players begin a scene from a fictional movie (title can be given by the audience). At any point, the Director can yell, "Cut!" and stop the action. He or she then asks the players to either redo the scene or continue, but to add more _____ (insert audience-suggested emotion, noun, etc.).

Skills: Scene Development, Spontaneity, Adaptability, Support Your Partner, and Listening.

Teaching Tips: As with the other scenic games, a solid base scene is the most important element. The timing of the "Cut" is what makes the game work. Look for times to heighten the scene, raise the stakes, etc. Too much cutting causes confusion, while not enough leaves the scene lacking variety and misses the crux of the game. Directors, remember that you are working to set your partners up for success, not to embarrass them for a cheap laugh.

Game: Evil Twin

Description: 3 players – The Good Twin, The Evil Twin, and the scene partner. The Good Twin and the scene partner begin a regular scene. At any point the Evil Twin can tap out the Good Twin and throw a wrench in the scene. The Evil Twin quickly steps out, while the Good Twin steps back in and tries to positively justify what happened. For example:

GT: "I can't wait to try the food at this restau-
    rant, Diane."
Diane: "Me either."
ET: (Tapping out GT) "Just lay off the cheddar bread-
    sticks this time. If you know what I mean."
Diane: "What are you trying to say?"
GT: "I hear the bread servers don't wash their
    hands. So I don't want you to get sick."

Skills: Justification, Scene Development, Spontaneity, Adaptability, Support Your Partner, and Listening.

Teaching Tips: As with Ding, the success of the game depends on the timing of the Evil Twin's interjections. Too many and the scene never develops, not enough and we are just watching a regular scene. The Evil Twin can do more than just say mean things. He or she can change plans, mess with the space, etc. For example, in the above the Evil Twin could propose to Diane, which would likewise throw a wrench in the scene.

Game: Siamese Twin

Description: 2 players. The audience selects a body part where the twins are adjoined, as well as an esteemed occupation. Each twin has an emergency to attend to on the opposite side of the room. They must each try to convince the other which situation is more important, while physically trying to attend to their emergency. The game ends when one of the twins succeeds by either convincing the other or physically moving them across the space.

Skills: Agreement, Support Your Partner, Listening, Justification, Physicality, and Scene Development.

Teaching Tips: This is not a competition! You aren't trying to win the game. You are playing a scene where each character has a specific want – you just so happen to be stuck together.

Game: Dual Situations

Description: 2–4 players. The audience gives the players a dramatic situation (death in the family, a hurricane just destroyed your home, etc.). The players then act out a scene using the dramatic situation. The audience then gives the players an everyday situation (coffee pot is empty). The players then replay the scene with the same intensity and focus, but change the situation.

Skills: Scene Development, Emotional Point of View, Character Development, Heightening, Agreement, Listening, and Support Your Partner.

Teaching Tips: Put the same honesty and intensity into both scenes – don't play the joke, play the emotional truth and let the situational change drive the humor.

Game: Dual Speak

Description: 5 players. One player is a talk-show host, the other four players split into two pairs. Each pair must speak as one, so it should seem like there are only three voices in the scene. The host can ask the pairs questions, or do whatever is necessary to make the pairs speak.

Skills: Agreement, Support Your Partner, Listening, Spontaneity, and Gagging Your Inner Critic.

Teaching Tips: The tendency is for one player to lead and the other to follow. Do your best to get them to speak as a pair – it is more enjoyable to watch (and play) when we truly don't know what is going to be said.

Game: Pyramid Freeze Tag

Description: 5 players. Player 1 begins a solo scene, making specific and active choices. After that scene has been established, Player 2 enters with a strong declaration and starts a completely new scene. After a set time, Player 3 will enter, creating a new scene and so on for Players 4 and 5. The players will then leave in reverse order, justifying their exits, causing each scene to return to the previous scene. The game ends when Player 1 wraps up his or her initial solo scene.

Skills: Active Choices, Scene Development, Character Development, Spontaneity, Attentiveness, Being in the Moment, Listening, Focus, and Support Your Partner.

Teaching Tips: Specific scenes are much easier to play and remember, rather than vague ones. Make sure to keep your characters distinct between scenes, to avoid causing yourself or your partner confusion.

Game: Sit, Stand, Lie Down

Descriptions: 3 players. At all times one player must be sitting, another standing, and another lying down. The players will be given either a relationship or location as a starting point from which to begin a scene. They must adjust their positions in accordance with one another as the scene progresses, maintaining the sit, stand, lie down rule.

Skills: Physicality, Attentiveness, Justification, Support Your Partner, Scene Development, Focus, and Spontaneity.

Teaching Tips: The justification of your movement is part of the scene; it is not independent of it. Move with intention, but be attentive of the movement of your partners as well. Creating a specific scene with character wants will be helpful throughout this process.

Game: Dubbing

Descriptions: 4 players. Two players act out a scene in gibberish while the other two players translate the scene for the audience.

Variation: The two translators may have their backs to the action and must blindly translate.

Skills: Agreement, Spontaneity, Physicality, Support Your Partner, and Justification.

Teaching Tips: Allow time for the translators to speak before moving on to the next line in gibberish. The responsibility of the movement of the scene lies in both the gibberish player's and the translator's hands. Each affects the other.

Game: Slips of Paper

Description: 3 players. Each player is given three slips of paper with a random audience-suggested phrase written on each. The players do not see/read the lines before the scene, and incorporate them throughout, justifying what they have just said.

Skills: Justification, Spontaneity, Agreement, Active Choices, Scene Development, and Listening.

Teaching Tips: When playing, try to avoid segues into your slip of paper with stock phrases such as "Well, my mom always said ... " "Let me read that sign ... " or "I once read a book that said ... ".

Game: Actor's Nightmare

Description: 2 players. Player 1 has a script in hand, from which they will take all of their lines. Player 2 has no script and must justify Player 1's lines throughout the scene.

Skills: Justification, Spontaneity, Agreement, Active Choices, Scene Development, and Listening.

Teaching Tips: Even though Player 1 has all of their lines, they must still be an active part of the scene. If the show is after a main stage production, it is typical to use that script for the game.

Game: He Said, She Said

Description: 2 players. Players perform a scene. Each line except the initiation has two parts. The first part must endow the other person with some sort of action, intention, etc. The second part would then be the "normal" part of the line. For example:

```
Player 1: "I want some milk."
Player 2: (endowment) "He said as he picked up a
          rusty knife. (normal) Is two percent okay?"
Player 1: (endowment) "She said, clearly hold-
          ing back tears. (normal) Oh yeah, I love
          two percent."
```

Players then take on the endowments and build them into the scene.

Skills: Listening, Spontaneity, Making Active Choices, Agreement, "Yes, And", Character Development, Support Your Partner, Scene Painting, and Scene Development.

Teaching Tips: Try to make the endowments a mixture of emotion, action, and intentions. It makes the game easier to play and more fun to watch. For more advanced players, there may come a time in the scene where you no longer have to endow every single line, but again, that's for really advanced players.

Group Games

Game: Beastie Boys

Description: Any number of players with a minimum of two teams, and a host. One player from each team is designated as the Rapper. The host solicits a one-syllable word from the audience, for example

132

"toe." Rapper 1 begins the game by using the word in a single line that matches the four-count rhythm. For instance, "I stubbed my foot, and I broke my—". Rapper 1's teammates then end the line with "toe." Rapper 2 must now come up with a phrase where the last word rhymes with "toe." Since his or her teammates must all correctly guess the rhyme, the Rapper needs to set up the rhyme. For instance, "I met Frosty, he's made of—", to which his or her teammates would say, "snow!" The Rappers then continue going back and forth until someone cannot rhyme. If a Rapper cannot come up with a rhyme, his or her teammates can't match the rhyme, or if a rhyme word is repeated, that Rapper is out and is replaced with a team member. If no one is being eliminated, the host can solicit a two or three-syllable word. It is up to the host to end the game.

Skills: Support Your Partner, Group Mind, Listening, Spontaneity, and Agreement.

Teaching Tips: The game is more important than an individual's desire to win. It is up to the discretion of the host if a player is out – sometimes the host will eliminate a player simply to keep the game moving.

Game: Photo Album

Description: Any number of players, with two players narrating the game. Two players have just returned from a fabulous trip and they are showing us their photo album. The two players begin describing an event, occurrence, etc. from the trip. They then set up the picture, for instance by saying, "Boy, we sure had a great time at Sandals Resort. Remember that pig roast, and the guy who set your skirt on fire?" The two players then say, "I think I have a picture of that. Let's see it in 3-2-1." While the two players are counting down 3-2-1, the other players must recreate the picture. The only time they are allowed to move is while the two players are counting down. While the players are in the picture tableau, the two narrators use the players' body language and location to describe the event in more detail. The game ends after we are shown three pictures.

Skills: Physicality, Spontaneity, Justification, "Yes, And", Agreement, Editing, and Listening.

Teaching Tips: Make sure that you don't spend too much time on one picture. Keep the game moving forward. If there is a big laugh or nice edit point in a picture, cut the scene and move to the next picture (even if you think you have something hilarious to add).

Game: Game-O-Matic

Description: Any number of players. The audience provides the players with four things: a name for the game; a goal to work toward; an obstacle to overcome; and how you win. The players then work as a unit to follow the guidelines of the game.

Skills: Group Mind, Support Your Partner, Agreement, Listening, Spontaneity, and Physicality.

Teaching Tips: The game can be anything. Remember that the audience is watching you, and you might find this game more helpful as a rehearsal exercise.

Game: Expert

Description: 1 player is an expert in an audience-suggested topic. All other players form two lines on opposite sides of the stage. Two players from each line step on stage. The expert begins lecturing to one group. While this is happening, the other group is physically mocking the expert in an attempt to make the other group laugh. When the expert turns around, the mocking players must freeze and attempt to look as neutral as possible. If the expert has any suspicions, he or she can kick the players out and the next two in line replace them.

Skills: Physicality, Spontaneity, Energy, Gag Your Inner Critic, and Support Your Partner.

Teaching Tips: The game is more important than the individual, so don't argue if the expert kicks you out. You will be caught – that is the fun of the game.

Energy Games

Game: Survivor

Description: 5 players. Each player is given a number between 1 and 5. They are given a task, quest or hunt. They then perform a highly physical scene carrying out their suggestion. At the end of the scene, an audience member or the host selects a number from a hat. That player leaves the scene, and the remaining four players must re-enact the scene incorporating all five of the original players. In other words, the player leaves the scene; his or her character does not. This process is repeated until one player must recreate the entire scene all by him or herself.

Skills: Attentiveness, Group Mind, Physicality, Spatial Awareness, Agreement, Scene Building, and Support Your Partner.

Teaching Tips: Not all players need to remain as one big group. If the scene requires a villain, one player should step out and play the villain. In other words, perform a scene with characters and actions, rather than an angry mob running around. The Buddy System is helpful, where two or three players sort of join forces, which can help control the chaos of five people all working independently.

Game: Sportscasters

Description: 4 players. Two players are announcing the competition; the other two are the contestants in said competition. The audience gives the players an everyday task that is then played out as an Olympic-style sport (e.g. brushing your teeth). The competitors begin the task, but do so in slow motion, obviously exaggerating the task to make it seem like it is physically and mentally demanding. The announcers narrate the action and help move the game along.

Skills: Physicality, Support Your Partner, Listening, and Agreement.

Teaching Tips: It is helpful to have one play-by-play announcer and one former competitor as an announcer who can provide expert insight into the event. There should be a give and take between the announcers and competitors – react to one another.

135

Game: Superheroes

Description: 4–5 players. The audience gives the players a world crisis that isn't really a crisis (such as the world is out of sharp cheddar cheese). The audience also names the first superhero. The first superhero sets up the situation. The second superhero enters the scene, and is named by the first superhero ("Thank God you're here, Dental Floss Man."). Upon arrival, the superhero must justify why he or she is perfect to help solve the crisis ("Don't worry, I'll use my super floss to cut the cheese, making it ridiculously sharp.") Each superhero enters in this manner – named by his or her predecessor and justifying his or her relevance. After all players have entered, the superheroes must leave in reverse order, justifying their exit.

Skills: Justification, Agreement, Physicality, Spontaneity, Listening, and Support Your Partner.

Teaching Tips: Make active choices and fully justify why each superhero is in the room. Own who you are.

Game: Half-Life

Description: 2–4 players. They act out a scene for one minute. Players then repeat the scene in 30 seconds trying to keep all of the dialogue, major physical action, and character wants as possible. The players then repeat the scene again in 15 seconds, 7 seconds, 3 seconds, and 1 second. You can either use the same players the entire time, or rotate players in to take on the characters in the scene.

Skills: Physicality, Agreement, Support Your Partner, Scene Development, Character Development, and Attentiveness.

Teaching Tips: A solid base scene is essential for the game to work. So make sure that there are distinct characters that want things from one another and are doing something physically. It's much easier (and more enjoyable) to edit a scene where something is happening than a vague, boring scene. Nobody wants to watch a crappy scene six times.

Game: Taxi

Description: 4 players. One player is a taxi cab driver. The audience gives the driver a quirk, who then incorporates the quirk into a character (e.g. quirk = itchy. So the driver is very fidgety and on edge). The driver then picks up the other three players one at a time. Each player chooses a quirk to enter the taxi with, and everyone in the taxi adapts to the quirk (so if someone enters and he or she is on fire, everyone in the cab is on fire). Once all four players are in the taxi, they then leave in reverse order until we are back to just the driver and his or her original quirk.

Skills: Justification, Spontaneity, Agreement, Group Mind, Listening, Attentiveness, and Support Your Partner.

Teaching Tips: Choose a specific character to play. There is a reason you are in the taxi and a specific place you *must* get to. Be mindful that four people acting crazy at the same time simply creates chaos, so share the focus.

Game: Grand Theft Auto

Description: 8 players in two groups of four. The audience will provide suggestions for adjective-noun combinations (e.g. floppy cucumbers). The first group is in the car when the driver looks out his or her window and sees a mob. He or she pulls out a slip of paper with one of the audience suggestions and announces, "Oh no, we're being

136

attacked by floppy cucumbers." At this point the other group become floppy cucumbers and hijack the car. The groups then simply take turns hijacking the car from one another.

Skills: Justification, Spontaneity, Physicality, Agreement, Group Mind, Listening, Attentiveness, and Support Your Partner.

Teaching Tips: Keep the game moving. Justify your reason for attack – you *must* get this car because of X.

Narrative Games

Game: Fortunately/Unfortunately

Description: 6–12 players with two narrators. One narrator is Fortunately, while the other is Unfortunately. The players are given the title of a story from the audience that has never been told before. Fortunately starts by introducing the main character and location. For example, "Fortunately, there was a young watermelon in the field." The other players would then act this out (playing either specific characters or scenery). Unfortunately agrees to that reality and continues the story. "Unfortunately, there was a Gallagher impersonator convention happening in that same field." The other players would then act this out as well. The story continues, one event at a time, with the actors physically bringing the story to life.

Skills: Listening, "Yes, And", Agreement, Physicality, Adaptability, Support Your Partner, Storytelling, and Spontaneity.

Teaching Tips: It is the narrator's job to move the story forward. This is most easily done by "Yes, And'ing" each other's statements. The actors don't simply react to what the narrators say, but may cause some of the action as well. Although the physical scenes may become hectic, everyone playing must constantly be listening to the narrator's directions, as you will have to adapt and adjust quickly.

Game: One-Word Story

Description: Any number of players. The players line up and are given the title of an original story suggested by the audience. The players must then tell the story one word at a time.

```
Player 1: Once
Player 2: upon
Player 3: a
Player 4: time
```

```
Player 5: there
Player 1: lived
Player 2: a
Player 3: floppy
Player 4: cucumber
Player 5: who
```

And so on ...

Variation: Try it with just two people. Tell a story together and aim to go fast enough that it sounds like just one person talking.

Skills: Listening, Agreement, Support Your Partner, Spontaneity, Group Mind, Storytelling, Being Present, and In The Moment.

Teaching Tips: There is not a leader and it is not helpful to try and preplan what you are going to say. Listen and stay in the moment, but do not try and control the flow of the story. It is a group effort. Keep a quick pace; the faster the story moves, the easier it is to react spontaneously.

Game: Conducted Story

Description: 4–8 players line up facing the conductor. They are given the title of an original story suggested by the audience. The players all tell the same story, but can only talk when pointed at by the conductor.

Variations:

*Story, Story, Die – once a player messes up, he or she is eliminated and must die via audience suggestion. For example, "Killed by butterflies!"

*Genres – each player is given a genre, magazine style, etc. that they must use to tell their section of the story.

Skills: Listening, Agreement, Storytelling, Support Your Partner, Spontaneity, Group Mind, Being Present, and In The Moment.

Teaching Tips: Remember that there is only one story being told. Do not completely change the style or the content (except in Genres, but even then the content should stay the same). In terms of elimination, winning is not as important as the story or game itself. If you are eliminated, don't fight it, die with dignity.

Game: Pen Name

Description: 4–10 players. Three players will narrate the story: one is the beginning, one is the middle, and one is the end. As they tell the story, the other players act out the story as in Fortunately/ Unfortunately. The middle storyteller simply tags out the beginning storyteller and takes over when he or she sees fit. The end storyteller likewise tags out the middle storyteller.

Skills: Storytelling, Listening, "Yes, And", Agreement, Physicality, Adaptability, Support Your Partner, and Spontaneity.

Teaching Tips: While it is the narrators who move the story forward, the actors don't simply react to what the narrators say, but may cause some of the action as well. Although the physical scenes may become hectic, everyone playing must constantly be listening to the narrator's directions, as you will have to adapt and adjust quickly.

Game: Documentary

Description: 2 players are given a suggestion from the audience. They then tell a story about some very interesting time in their lives. For instance, they might tell a story about how they got engaged, or the time they wrestled a dinosaur, etc. The topic is less important than the fact that it is a shared story.

Variation: Compliments – each person should say something nice or flattering about the other person as a way to build the story. Accept the compliment, build upon it, and then give one to your partner. "Yes, And" your little heart out.

Skills: Listening, "Yes, And", Storytelling, Support Your Partner, Agreement, and Group Mind.

Teaching Tips: The joy of the game is watching the two people interact. Create a character that has very specific feelings about the person sitting next to them, as well as very specific feelings about the story they are telling. No matter how ridiculous the topic of the story, be honest and sincere about what happened and your emotions.

Game: Poet's Corner

Description: 4 players and a host. The audience gives the players a suggestion. Each player then develops a poet persona based on the suggestion, and spontaneously delivers a poem on the subject.

Skills: Spontaneity, Gagging Your Inner Critic, Focus, and Being in the Moment.

Teaching Tips: While it might be alluring to develop a persona beforehand, the real fun of the game is letting the suggestion inspire your creativity.

Game: Did You Say?

Description: 1 player. The audience suggests a topic for the speaker to discuss. Other players can join the audience for this game. The speaker begins talking, and at any point an audience member or player can interrupt and ask, "I'm sorry, did you say _____?" For instance, the speaker says, "So it is widely known that bananas are a common cure for bug bites." Audience member: "I'm sorry, did you say bug bites?" At this point the speaker must correct him or herself by substituting a similar-sounding word or phrase. For instance, "No I didn't. I said shrug fights. Which are very common in the Midwest." The speaker then uses the correction as a catalyst for further discussion until he or she is interrupted again.

Skills: Spontaneity, "Yes, And", Agreement, Attentiveness, Storytelling, Listening, Justification, and Being in the Moment.

Teaching Tips: You are an expert on the topic – no matter what it is. Speak with confidence. For the players in the audience: don't overdo it. Find the right balance to allow the speaker a chance to talk and justify his or her correction (which is where a lot of the humor resides).

Ask The Audience Games

Game: Buddha

Description: 3 players and a host. The players line up one behind the other – the first is sitting, the second is kneeling, and the third is standing. The host will solicit questions from the audience. For each question, the players answer one word at a time. When they feel that they have answered the question, they will say in turn, Player 1: "Buddha." Player 2: "Has." Player 3: "Spoken." The host will then justify Buddha's answer. Generally the players answer 3–5 questions depending on time.

Skills: Justification, Spontaneity, Group Mind, Agreement, Listening, and Being Present in the Moment.

Teaching Tips: The Buddha answers should not just be random. They should have some nugget of truth in them that the host then plays with and justifies. Buddha players need to take themselves seriously. It undercuts your authority if you are laughing at what you or your partners are saying.

Game: Good, Bad, Ugly

Description: 3 players and a host. One player is giving good advice, one player is giving bad advice, and one player is giving the absolute worst possible advice. The host will solicit questions from the audience. For each question, the players then answer in order, starting with good advice and ending with the worst advice.

Skills: Spontaneity, Group Mind, "Yes, And", Agreement, Listening, and Being Present in the Moment.

Teaching Tips: Since the Ugly advice is supposed to be the worst advice in the world, the first two players must then work to help set up the Ugly player. The Bad advice especially shouldn't trump the worst advice. Again, the game is more important than a funny joke you might have.

Game: Gibberish Translator

Description: 2 players and a host. One player is an expert in a particular field or topic (suggested by the audience). This player, however, does not speak English. He or she speaks a gibberish language. Therefore, one player serves as a translator. The host will solicit questions from the audience. The expert will answer in gibberish (physicality is always a plus), and the translator will convey the answer in English.

Skills: Justification, Spontaneity, "Yes, And", Agreement, Listening, and Being Present in the Moment.

Teaching Tips: This sounds silly, but vary the gibberish – both in length of answers and the literal sound. The expert doesn't have to do full out pantomime, but it is funnier if there is some sort of physicality that the translator must also justify.

Game: Audience Text

Description: 2–4 players and a host. Ask an audience member for their mobile phone. Open up their texting app/device. One player then uses the audience member's text messages as his or her dialogue. The other player(s) improvise dialogue and must justify the text lines.

Skills: Justification, Spontaneity, "Yes, And", Agreement, Listening, and Being Present in the Moment.

Teaching Tips: It should go without saying, but don't read any text messages that will be mortifyingly embarrassing for the audience member. We want to laugh with them, not at them.

One-Liner Games

Game: World's Worst

Description: Any number of players form a line. The audience will suggest an occupation, event, or any other general topic. It is up to the players to then give an example of the world's worst version of that specific thing. For example, if the suggestion is "birth control," a player might step out and say "Don't worry, I'm already pregnant."

Skills: Spontaneity, Support Your Partner, Listening, and Gag Your Inner Critic.

Teaching Tips: There is nothing worse than an empty stage. So even if you have nothing, sometimes it's your job to buy time for your teammates. For the host, do your best to cut each suggestion on a high note (or if it is dying, as quickly as possible). If a line kills, cut it. Even if your boyfriend steps out and has something he thinks is funny to say. Again, the game is more important than the individual. Listen to what your teammates say – nobody wants to hear the same joke twice (or ten times).

142

Game: 185

Description: Any number of players form a line. The audience gives a suggestion of pretty much any noun. The lines follow the below pattern. In this example, our suggestion is "computers."

Player 1: "185 computers walk into a bar. The bartender says, 'We don't serve your kind.' The computers say, 'My motherboard is going to hear about this!'"

Skills: Spontaneity, Support Your Partner, Listening, and Gag Your Inner Critic.

Teaching Tips: Again, an empty stage is the enemy … and pretty much everything else from World's Worst.

Game: I Like My …

Description: Any number of players form a line. The audience gives a suggestion of pretty much anything. The lines follow the below pattern. In this example, our suggestion is "pets."

Player 1: "I like my men (or women) like I like my pets: domesticated."

Skills: Spontaneity, Support Your Partner, Listening, and Gag Your Inner Critic.

Teaching Tips: The same as above. This game in particular walks a fine line between funny and offensive. Remember that you are a team, so if someone says something particularly lewd (and/or offensive), the audience might need a break. So don't be afraid to say something that isn't at all sexual. For instance, "I like my men like I like my pets: helping the blind."

143

Long Form Improv Games

Long form improv is the other main performance genre of improvisation, and has become much more popular in the last decade with most professional theaters (save ComedySportz and Theatresports) performing long form improv. As noted in the Introduction, long form improv is a scenic-based style where humor arises from relationships and connections. Each form/structure in this section tends to be between 15 and 30 minutes long.

A note about *editing* ... Most short form games have a rather obvious ending. In long form, however, there usually isn't a set ending either to a structure or an individual scene. Therefore it becomes the responsibility of the players to edit. Generally, a scene is edited when it has hit a high point, sufficiently played the game of the scene, set up an interesting second scene/beat – think commercial break – or is simply dying and needs to be put out of its misery. A good rule of thumb is to edit a scene before you think, "Gosh, somebody should edit this scene." To get started, here are a few basic edits. There are many more styles, but these five are fairly standard/common.

1. Swipe/Sweep Edit: The most basic edit. When a player feels like a scene needs to be edited, they simply run in front of the scene (some teams have the players say "Swoosh!" as they cross). This edit clears the stage and gives us a "blank slate" for the next scene. Either the player who edited or another teammate will then immediately begin a new scene.

2. Tag-Out Edit: This edit can be used to end a scene, or to provide a quick tangent to heighten the stakes of the scene. To do a Tag-Out a player gets on stage and tags out someone in the scene. That player then leaves the stage. The players left on stage remain the same characters. This edit provides a quick way to explore the dynamics of a character or situation. The tagged-out player must remain alert as often a Tag-Out edit is done as part of a scene rather than as an end to a scene. For instance, my character might say, "I have no luck with women." Another player can Tag-Out my scene partner and then do a quick scene demonstrating my character's lack of luck with women, at which point the tagged-out player would then tag back in.

3. Swinging Door Edit: This edit is similar in intention to the Tag-Out. To execute a Swinging Door edit, a third player will temporarily interrupt a two-person scene by grabbing and literally

spinning one of the players already in the scene, offer a quick initiation (with a short scene that may or may not follow), and then swing them back into the original scene. The Swinging Door scene is in a new time or place, usually in the past but not always (the original scene is essentially on pause). The point is to highlight the game of the scene, to heighten the situation, or to generally reveal new information in the current scene to heighten or further the comedic situation. Swinging Door scenes can ping-pong back and forth between the original scene and the new scene, or simply be a quick in and out. The major difference between this and a Tag-Out is that a Swinging Door edit/scene is generally understood by all to be a very short interruption to the original scene, whereas a Tag-Out can take us to a totally new scene. Tag-Outs can also be done as a run by a series of players (for the above example of the "I have no luck with women," we might have three Tag-Outs with various women that build in awfulness), whereas there is usually only one Swinging Door edit per scene, though it is certainly possible to do a Swinging Door edit with each character on stage as opposed to only one.

4. Cut-To Edit: To execute a Cut-To edit, a player says, "Cut to _____." The players then immediately move to the new scene. For instance, two players are doing a scene about a playground bully, when another players says, "Cut to the bully being confronted by his parents." Or, "Cut to the teacher's lounge." As demonstrated, the Cut-To can either involve players in the scene or take us to a new scene. This edit is a lot of fun, but be wary of overusing it.

5. Internal Edit: While someone not in the scene usually makes the other four edits, an internal edit is done by one of the players currently in the scene. An internal edit is done by one of the players making a clear, clean, and sharp change to signify he or she is moving to a new scene. It can be a vocal and/or physical change; you can step out and start a monologue or begin scene painting a new scene, or simply give a new line of dialogue.

The other big spot for editing your show is at the end. There are two main options for ending a show. If you are in a theater with a light board and you have an operator you trust, let them black out the show. This takes the pressure off you as a performer, but it also puts

146

a lot of pressure on the technician to get the ending right so make sure he or she really understands the form you are doing. The other option is to self-edit by simply breaking out of the action and saying "Thank you! That's our set!" The self-edit option is a little clumsier than a blackout and puts the burden on you as a performer, though the ending is usually pretty obvious once you gain some experience. The third option is having an ending that is so obviously the ending that nothing needs to be said and the audience simply begins clapping and cheering.

Along with editing, another skill that is more common to long form is using and reusing information. Often called a callback or connection, let's generically call it a *second beat*. This is when a player uses information from a previous scene in a later scene, whether it is a returning character or theme. There are three major ways that improvisers "pull" material: character pull, tangential pull, and thematic pull. A character pull follows one or both of the characters from the original scene; a tangential pull takes something from the original scene that is somewhat related (perhaps there is an object or place mentioned) and we use that information to start a new scene; and a thematic pull uses the theme from the original scene/monologue and pulls out its theme or game to start a new scene.

The original source can be from the opening in the form of a monologue(s) or group scene or even simply a word, or it can be the first beat of a Harold, or scene in a LaRonde. Pretty much every long form structure requires some sort of callback, connection, or pull. So let's look at a hypothetical "original" scene and then look at a sample character pull, tangential pull, and thematic pull.

Original Scene: Harry and Eleanor are on a cruise celebrating their twenty-fifth anniversary. Eleanor finally admits that she cheated on Harry 15 years ago. He is relieved because he knew, but because he's so non-confrontational he didn't want to accuse her ... plus he knows that it was a stupid mistake.

Character Pull Options: A scene between Eleanor and her lover; a scene between Harry and Eleanor's lover; a scene between Harry and Eleanor on their tenth anniversary; a scene between Harry and Eleanor the night before or after she cheats. There are numerous other options, but these are a few of the "better" options.

Tangential Pull Options: Pretty much anything happening on the cruise – if it is a scene that is happening at the same time as the original or can relate to it in any way, all the better. One way to think about the tangential pull is to "pull" the world from the first scene. Let us see how other people in that world work, or how unknowingly Eleanor and Harry impact others. It's possible to create a tangential thematic pull as well – perhaps the captain of the ship has some long-held secret he needs to reveal to the crew that they knew all along. Here we are pulling the world from the original scene as well as the theme of long-held "secrets."

Thematic Pull Options: Without really seeing the scene, it's difficult to really nail down the theme, but I like to try and put the theme into one word or phrase. For this scene, the theme might be "forgiveness," but you could also argue that it's "weakness." In either case, some thematic options: a scene where a friend reveals some very bad news that is taken really well; a non-confrontational lawyer scene; a long-held secret that is really trivial but is responded to as though it was the end of the world (because the original took a big betrayal and said it was okay, let's flip the script and have a character get really mad that you took a piece of gum from her purse in 1994).

With any pull you are looking for what worked in the original scene. What was fun? What did the audience enjoy? If you are a big game of the scene person, you are looking for the game and then playing it in a new situation/scenario. That's what you want to emphasize in a second beat. You are looking to continue what was fun – so be sure that you aren't too concerned with plot. The fun of our original scene was in not only forgiving what may seem to be unforgivable, but for the aggrieved to be relieved by it. The second beat should be looking for situations to heighten that sense of relief in terms of character, location/context (where would it be even more absurd to be relieved by an admission of guilt – court, heaven, etc.), or by making the behavior universal (Harry lets people take advantage of him no matter the situation). Whatever you choose, doing pulls or second beats is a great way to emphasize what is working in your show and to follow the fun.

And of course no long form would be complete without *group scenes*. We've spent a lot of time focused on two-person scenes, but as I'm sure you noticed in short form, improv has a lot of group scenes. A good long form performance is going to have a variety of scenes – both in terms of length, energy, content, and number of performers. Group scenes can be tricky if everyone pushes their own agenda instead of applying the basic rule of improv – play along. If you approach them correctly, group scenes can be a lot of fun; if you don't

148

they can be a cluster-fuck that ruins your show. There are really three types of group scenes.

1. The Team: In this type of group scene everyone agrees to one idea and builds it together. For example: "It's cold out." "It's so cold I might lose a finger." "I've only felt this cold once in my life – the time my dog died." "When it gets this cold you might as well just give up." And so on. Everyone is agreeing that it is cold, and then building and heightening.
2. The Outsider: In this type of group scene there is one person that is different. Somebody is Katniss Everdeen. You are the one smart guy at the meeting, or the one inmate who doesn't love prison, or the nun looking for adventure. You are the one who thinks your group can beat the cold. In essence, this type of scene becomes a big two-person scene: the group and the outsider.
3. The Jets and The Sharks: In this type of group scene, players separate into two groups. The husbands and the wives, the players and the refs, the students and the teachers. Within each group your only job is to support the group's point of view. Again, this in essence becomes a two-person scene.

149

Long Form Contents

Openings

Patterns
Voicemail
Monologues
Organic

Long Form Structures

The Harold
Montage
The Car
The Weinberg
LaRonde
Deconstruction
Audience Interview
Murder Mystery
WeirDass
Armando Diaz and ASSSSCAT 3000!!!!
Chain Smoking (or Associative Scenes)
The Living Room
The Movie
Go

Long Form Contents

Openings

Most long form structures use an opening. Since you generally are only getting one audience suggestion at the top of the form, the opening serves to help give you inspiration. The opening works to: 1) generate material; 2) foster group mind and build connections between the players; and 3) let the audience into the creative process. The opening prompts both the audience and the players on the piece about to unfold. Much of the comedy in a long form is based on connections and callbacks, and many of those initial seeds are planted in the opening. Remember that this is often the first impression you are making on your audience, so make sure that your opening is *performative*. You don't want to just stand in a line and neutrally say some words. While your main goal is to generate ideas, you need to keep in mind that someone is watching.

There are numerous forms and structures for openings, but here are a few to consider.

Opening: Patterns

Description: Combining word association with pattern-making skills, this opener works to create ideas and premises from a single suggestion by building a pattern. Generally you want to have three loops of information. A loop is complete when the pattern returns to the original suggestion. For more info on how these work, see "Patterns" and "A–C Patterns" in Section III, or check out the *UCB Comedy Improvisation Manual*.

Opening: Voicemail

Description: The team gets an audience suggestion. Then one player steps out to leave a voicemail recording message – "Hi, this is Beverly. Leave me a message and I'll get back to you!" The rest of the team then takes turns leaving Beverly messages. Be sure not to simply follow one plot with the messages, but to make them varied. For example:

```
"Hi Beverly. This is Brad. You didn't show for
    our date. What's up?"
"Hi Beverly. This is your Mother. My foot is doing
    that thing again where it swells up and I
    can't walk. I don't want to bother you."
```

"Hi Beverly. Sheila from work. Thanks so much
for getting that quarterly report done for
me. Coney Island was great!"
"Hi Beverly. It's your mother's foot. Listen,
if you could just call her back that would
be great."

And so on …

Opening: Monologues

Description: Based on the audience suggestion, each member of the group takes turns telling short *personal* monologues that are *true*. Again, each monologue should be unique and focused on generating new ideas rather than rehashing something we've heard in a previous monologue. Monologues can be done in character, but these are much more difficult and less fruitful in terms of generating scenic material.

Opening: Organic

Description: An organic opener can pretty much take any form. It can combine elements of numerous openers: Patterns, Invocations, Voicemails, Physical Movements, Word Associations … pretty much anything. The idea is that the team doesn't plan the structure of the opening and lets the action organically emerge. This opening can be very satisfying if done well, but obviously has the potential to be slow, boring for the audience, and not very generative.

Long Form Structures

Structure: The Harold

Description: The granddaddy of all long form structures. 6–12 players. The basic structure begins with three unrelated scenes that are revisited in some form two more times each for a total of nine scenes. Humor comes from connections, callbacks, and relationships. If you can do a Harold, you can pretty much do any long form since the Harold requires/tests all of the skills needed for long form: scene building, relationships, game of the scene, callbacks, connections, group mind, and of course, listening! The basic structure is as follows:

Opening
1A 1B 1C (The First Beat)
Group Game
2A 2B 2C (The Second Beat)
Group Game
3A 3B 3C (The Third Beat)
Ending

The Opening can consist of any number of things, such as a word association, monologues, physical movement, invocation, or any other group activity. The goal of the opening is to generate ideas. The opening is similar to the overture in a musical – it will provide the base for what is to come.

The First Beat (1A, 1B, 1C) establishes the major relationships, characters, and locations. Each scene should be completely disconnected from the other two, but all three scenes should be pulling some sort of inspiration from the opening. Generally these are two-character scenes that run about 2 minutes. Think about a teepee – the three stakes on the ground have to be very far apart for the top to come together tightly.

The First Group Game is designed to bring the entire ensemble together again to explore the themes developed in the first beat and reestablish the group mind. The game can be anything and take any form. Note: Game does not mean play a short form game.

The Second Beat (2A, 2B, 2C) explores and heightens the first beat. So 2A is related to 1A, 2B to 1B, and 2C to 1C. The second beat can follow the narrative of the first beat, follow one character, follow the game of the scene (in a new situation), or thematically explore the idea(s) established in the first beat. Players should look to heighten something specific from the first beat – whether that is plot or theme. At this point players should not try and force any connections.

*Note: if you appear in 1A, then whenever you appear in the A beat (1A, 2A, 3A) you generally play the same character. If you are in the B or C beat, however, you can either play the same character or be someone different.

The Second Group Game is designed to bring the entire ensemble together again to explore the themes, and to reconnect with the original audience suggestion. Like the first game, this game can take many forms. Ideally the second game acts as a springboard into the third beat.

The Third Beat (3A, 3B, 3C) is where characters, relationships, locations, plot lines, themes and everything else comes together. Connections should arise organically, rather than be forced upon the action. In a traditional Harold, the third beat contains three scenes. However, it is more than acceptable to have either one large group scene, or a string of short scenes. Whatever structure works best to make connections.

The Ending – if an ending does not emerge in the third beat, players can continue with a string of very short scenes that work to tie everything together.

Example Harold!

The audience suggestion is "sleeve." For the opener, let's say the group does monologues.

> Player 1: A monologue about how he doesn't like to wear sleeves when he shaves.
> Player 2: A monologue about her experience getting waxed before her sister's wedding. The cosmetologist was a little tipsy.
> Player 3: A monologue about finding out that his girlfriend is pregnant the same day the frozen yogurt place down the street opened. Not sure which he's more excited about.
> Player 4: A monologue about the time she got bit by a cow on a school field trip to a local farm.

Player 5: A monologue about growing up in the Bible Belt and later realizing that some people haven't read the Bible.

Player 6: A monologue about the time he went to the haberdashery to get his pants lengthened, but the tailor kept pushing Cuban cigars on him to the point where he just bought them to get the guy to shut up.

1A: Two cows, who are sisters, are on a field trip to the city. The older sister wants to stay and make a new life in the big city, while the younger sister thinks they should head back home where they belong. *Idea pulled from Player 4's monologue.*

1B: An author is at a book signing for his debut novel, which is a kids' illustrated version of the Bible. Jesus is next in line to get his book signed. He's got one of those pens with multiple-colored inks (you know, because he's Jesus). The author is more excited about the pen than Jesus, who is totally fan-girling over the book, but ultimately gets a little pissed that the author is more impressed with the pen than with the fact that Jesus is standing in front of him. *Ideas pulled from Player 3's and Player 5's monologues.*

1C: We are at a home birth. The dad-to-be is really nervous and feels like they should be at the hospital. The mom-to-be is all about being natural. The midwife is a little tipsy and sells make-up as an independent contractor, which she keeps pushing on the mom. The scene is cut right before the baby is born and as both the midwife and dad-to-be pass out. *Ideas pulled from Player 2's and Player 6's monologues.*

1st Group Game: Everyone comes out on stage. They form the shape of a swollen udder, with each player becoming a nipple. The back-left nipple has been lacking in milk production – "I'm in the back so it's hard to get a good grip" – so the other nipples want to kick him out.

2A: It's five years later. The older sister cow has opened a nail salon and is very successful, but also very lonely, though she doesn't want to let on. Her younger sister, her husband, and two calves have come to visit with a last-minute plea to come back home to save the family farm since she's the only one with enough money to get them out of trouble. *This is an example of a narrative time-dash second beat. We move forward in time (time-dash) while following and forwarding the plot of 1A.*

155

2B: Kindergarten book club meeting to discuss the "Kidz Bible." They are kids, but they comment on the book in a very adult way – "I found the scratch and sniff stickers to be a tad offensive." "I found the Noah's Ark coloring sheet to be particularly difficult. So many lines to stay inside." "I really liked the ending, but now I can't get out of this existential funk." *This is an example of a thematic/tangential second beat, in this case taking an item from 1B, the Kidz Bible, and making it the center of 2B.*

2C: We are at a home burial ... as in Grandpa is being buried in his backyard. The priest is trying to talk Grandma out of it, but she insists – "When the kids are playing in the sandbox, I want them to know they are playing on top of their grandfather." The various family members all object, while Grandma finds more ways to justify the at-home burial. She also sells perfume and keeps pushing it on the priest – "It'll be great for your incense during mass." *This is an example of a game-of-the-scene second beat, where the game is "things that used to always be done at home, but are now usually done in an offsite facility."*

2nd Group Game: Everyone comes out on stage and begins doing a mundane task. To complete the task they must rip off their sleeves. Players are drinking a glass of water, brushing teeth, tying shoes, and milking a cow – the players quickly reassume the swollen udder from game one, which propels us into the third beat.

3A/B/C: The cows are back on the farm. The younger sister is giving birth, but like in City Slickers, the calf is breeched. They need to get it out now! The dad cow passes out. The kindergarten book club is on a field trip to the farm and is witnessing the chaos. One of the kids happens to be the daughter of the midwife from 1C. "I've seen my mother do this a thousand times!" She takes out a bottle of Robutissin. "Is that for the cow?" "No, it's for me. But if anybody wants some I'm selling it three bucks a bottle, five bucks for two." She downs the whole bottle, rips off her sleeves – in solidarity her classmates do the same – and with the help of the older sister cow, she births the breeched calf. They then swaddle the calf in the children's ripped-off sleeves, forming a Mary, Joseph, Baby Jesus tableau. BLACKOUT. *This is an example of a single scene third beat where everything comes together in one big scene rather than three (or more) separate scenes.*

Skills: Scene Development, Support Your Partner, Group Mind, Listening, Justification, Reincorporation, Agreement, Editing ... and pretty much everything.

156

Teaching Tips: Focus on strong first beats that have solid relationships – it's always best if the characters have a shared history. Even if the scene is between two cows. That scene is really about the relationship between two sisters – one wants to move on and the other is afraid of losing her sister. It just happens to be between two cows.

Don't rush connections. Let the first beat be as far apart as possible. It is actually easier to connect diverse scenes than it is to connect three very similar scenes.

Don't rely on plot. The Harold can be executed with no plot at all, so don't overlook themes – themes can raise the work to another level. In your second beats look to make thematic connections, or to play the game of the scene (in a new situation), rather than solely trying to advance the plot.

As with any long form structure, variety is key. That means different energies, relationships, locations, characters, time frames, time lengths, points of view, and emotions.

Don't be discouraged; you will fail at times, and that's okay. Learn from your mistakes and move forward.

Practice writing out Harolds. Get in groups of two or three and write out a Harold together. Then do it with your whole group. It'll give you practice working with others and making connections without the pressure of performing it, and will help to solidify the form (it'll also help you if you want to write for television some day).

The Harold can also be performed without relying rigidly on the above structure. Many define a Harold simply as a long form structure that features callbacks, recycling, and connections.

Structure: Montage

Description: 3–10 players. While the Harold has a rather firm structure, a Montage is simply a collection of scenes. While there can be callbacks and recurring characters, a traditional Montage is more akin to a collage of different scenes. There really are no guidelines other than to keep things diverse. You can put different variations into effect, such as having all the scenes at the same location (e.g. a high school – though try to think outside of the box so we don't just see 20 student–teacher scenes).

Skills: Scene Development, Support Your Partner, Group Mind, Listening, Justification, Reincorporation, Agreement, Editing, and Spontaneity.

Teaching Tips: Players tend to try and develop a plot. While that is okay, try and get them to more fully explore themes. Again, the basic rules of scene work will go a long way toward the success of the form. Really focus on strong scene work and relationships and remember to think about variety – in terms of topics, pace, rhythm, environments, characters, and energies.

Structure: The Car

Description: 4 players. Set up four chairs as if it's a car. The idea is that there are four people in the car who know each other driving to some event (wedding, funeral, party, sporting event, reunion, etc.) There will be three beats of this scene. The second and third beats should progress in time instead of picking up exactly where the previous beat ended. The third beat is relatively short, more akin to a blackout style scene that wraps everything up in a couple lines.

Skills: Scene Development, Support Your Partner, Group Mind, Listening, Justification, Reincorporation, Agreement, Editing, and Character Development.

Variation: Combining this form with a Montage or other loosely structured form can help provide a through line to an otherwise free-form structure.

Teaching Tips: In many ways you are simply doing one thread of a Harold. Focus on building a strong relationship in the first beat, heightening and exploring in the second, and resolving/wrapping up in the third. This structure is also all about plot, so don't worry about following a thematic second beat. Again, really focus on the relationships between the four people in the car. They are all there for a reason and they are together for a reason. Scenes tend to turn into three against one – that's okay, just remember that allegiances often change moment to moment and beat to beat.

Structure: The Weinberg

Description: 4–6 players. One player is designated as "The Berger." This player is in every scene, but plays a different character with each scene partner. For example, The Berger is always Stay-at-Home Joe whenever he is in a scene with Player 1, but is never Stay-at-Home Joe in any other scene. Much like a Harold, there are three beats, but the individual scenes do not connect (they can, but that isn't the goal). The first beat establishes the relationships, the second beat heightens

158

the stakes, and the third beat wraps up the encounter. Here is the basic structure:

Player 1 and The Berger
Player 2 and The Berger (The Berger is a different character)
Player 3 and The Berger (Again, The Berger is a different character)
Player 1 and The Berger (The Berger is the same character as in the first scene)
Player 2 and The Berger (The Berger is the same character as in the second scene)
Player 3 and The Berger (The Berger is the same character as in the third scene)
Player 1 and The Berger (The Berger is the same character as in the first scene)
Player 2 and The Berger (The Berger is the same character as in the second scene)
Player 3 and The Berger (The Berger is the same character as in the third scene)

Skills: Scene Development, Support Your Partner, Group Mind, Listening, Justification, Reincorporation, Agreement, Editing, and Character Development.

Teaching Tips: Remember that "The Berger" is in multiple scenes so having a clearly defined relationship with stakes will make it easier for that person to jump between scenes. Obviously with more players, be aware of the time. Don't force connections. You are using a similar structure to a Harold, but you are not trying to connect all the stories/themes together. If connections organically emerge that's great, but that isn't the goal.

Structure: LaRonde

Description: 6–10 players. This form is all about exploring character, and as such each player will play one character in two different scenes. The basic form is below:

Scene 1: Player 1 and Player 2
Scene 2: Player 2 (same character as in Scene 1) and Player 3
Scene 3: Player 3 (same character as in Scene 2) and Player 4
Scene 4: Player 4 (same character as in Scene 3) and Player 5

Scene 5: Player 5 (same character as in Scene 4) and Player 6
Scene 6: Player 6 (same character as in Scene 5) and Player 1 (same character as in Scene 1)

The idea is to see one character in two different situations. For example, in scene 1, Player 1 is a mother dealing with her rambunctious teenage son (Player 2) and getting nowhere. In scene 2, the rambunctious teenage son is comforting his girlfriend (Player 3) who just found out she didn't get into Harvard and he did. And so on ...

Skills: Character Development, Scene Development, Support Your Partner, Group Mind, Listening, Justification, Reincorporation, Agreement, and Editing.

Teaching Tips: The key to a successful LaRonde is strong character. When entering a new scene it is great to heighten another character, but remember to arm yourself. If you don't have anything you want and only focus on the other character, then the next player in line has nothing to heighten for the next scene.

LaRonde can be an effective way to practice 2nd beats of a Harold. If I were going to do a 2A based on this scene with this character, what would I do? The form can be standalone, in which case the scenes need a bit more time, or it can be used as an opener for a Harold. A team could also perform a series of scenes using the LaRonde characters.

Structure: Deconstruction

Description: 6–12 players. A traditional Deconstruction features one base scene from which every other scene is pulled. To end the structure, the original scene is replayed in light of everything that has happened. In other words, we have an initial scene that is then deconstructed by everything that follows. It can be helpful to think of the first scene as 1A in a Harold, and every other scene as a 2A that directly relates to the initial scene. Think of a bicycle wheel. The first scene is the hub, and every other scene is a spoke. The end scene then works like the tire to hold the wheel together.

The initial scene in a Deconstruction tends to be longer than a normal scene. It also features more storytelling, references to the past, and other characters than a traditional scene. Remember, this scene is in many ways acting as your opener, so you need a lot of ideas to sustain the form.

Skills: Scene Development, Support Your Partner, Group Mind, Listening, Justification, Reincorporation, Agreement, Editing, and Making the Unexpected Choice.

Teaching Tips: You really need strong scenes (especially early on) for a Deconstruction to work. Try to avoid plot in subsequent scenes, and instead use details in the previous scene as inspiration for characters or the scene itself.

Structure: Audience Interview

Description: 6–12 players. An audience member volunteers to share the details of his or her life. One player interviews the audience member, trying to get both the mundane and any odd or unusual happenings (be wary of time). Find out what the person does for a living (or their major), oddities from childhood, ask about their parents or siblings or friends. Let the interview flow organically, but remember that the interview is your opener. You want a variety of ideas, not just one long story.

After the interview, the players then use the interview as inspiration for scenes, heightening various situations and pointing out the absurd. Do not simply recreate what the audience member said. Use it as inspiration as you would any opener. Build on those stories and ideas and take them to new places. Look for humorous premises, games, or any unusual aspect that you can use to launch a scene.

Skills: Scene Development, Support Your Partner, Group Mind, Listening, Justification, Reincorporation, Agreement, and Making the Unexpected Choice.

Teaching Tips: Keep the interview about five minutes (assuming a half-hour set). Likewise, keep the scenes moving quickly and develop games as you go. Bear in mind that the audience has heard the same info you have, so don't simply repeat it. As with all audience games, your job is to make the participant look great.

Structure: Murder Mystery

Description: 5–10 players. There has been a murder; however, the game does not stop. One player is the Detective trying to solve the case, one player is the victim, three players are the possible suspects, and the other players fill in the gaps. The audience picks a player they would like to die (which is always fun). The following is the basic structure:

1. The Detective gives a monologue at the scene of the crime, identifying the body, endowing him or her with various traits, and describing how the victim might have died.

2. The next three scenes are with the potential suspects. Each suspect does a scene with the victim in which a possible motive arises. For example, the victim owns a donut shop, and one of the suspects was recently fired.
3. The Detective then gives another monologue that both recaps the suspects and adds new information about them.
4. The next three scenes again feature the suspects and again heighten their motives.
5. The Detective then interrogates the suspects, trying to get them to confess. Each time the Detective says, "I know you killed him, and this is how you did it!" At which point the suspect then acts out the murder. Two of the three deny it while the third admits his or her crime.

Skills: Scene Development, Support Your Partner, Group Mind, Listening, Justification, Reincorporation, Agreement, Editing, and Making the Unexpected Choice.

Teaching Tips: The game works best if everyone is heightening everything. Complicate the situation.

Structure: WeirDass

Description: 6–12 players. Stephanie Weir and Bob Dassie originally developed this form. Two players get an audience suggestion and then begin telling a joint story as though they are being interviewed for a documentary film. This will serve as a pseudo-opener and inspire a set of three independent scenes. Then two more players will begin a second documentary-style story (it is also acceptable to return to the original couple). Three more scenes follow, then another documentary, and three more scenes. Usually the scenes are unconnected, but there is certainly no rule against making callbacks or connections between scenes. After the three sets are done, some teams then do a string of scenes that begin to connect all of the threads together. So, the form looks like this:

1st Documentary Story
Scene 1 (inspired by documentary story 1)
Scene 2 (inspired by documentary story 1, but unrelated to Scene 1)
Scene 3 (inspired by documentary story 1, but unrelated to Scene 1 or 2)
2nd Documentary Story
Scene 4 (inspired by documentary story 2)

Scene 5 (inspired by documentary story 2, but unrelated to Scene 4)
Scene 6 (inspired by documentary story 2, but unrelated to Scene
    4 or 5)
3rd Documentary Story
Scene 7 (inspired by documentary story 3)
Scene 8 (inspired by documentary story 3, but unrelated to Scene 7)
Scene 9 (inspired by documentary story 3, but unrelated to Scene
    7 or 8)

Optional string of scenes connecting everything together.

Skills: Scene Development, Support Your Partner, Group Mind, Listening, Justification, Reincorporation, Agreement, Editing, Story-telling, and Making the Unexpected Choice.

Teaching Tips: The documentary-style monologues are used to inspire the scenes. Like with Deconstruction and other forms, take an element from the story to springboard into a new scene. We don't want to see you simply act out what the storytellers said. As noted, the amount of connectivity in the structure is up to the group.

Structure: Armando Diaz and ASSSSCAT 3000!!!!

Description: 6–12 players with either one player from the group (Armando) or an invited guest (ASSSSCAT) acting as monologist. The form starts with the monologist soliciting an audience suggestion. This can either be one word, or quite often is three unrelated ideas, objects, etc. that serve as inspiration. At any point in the monologue, a player can edit and begin a scene inspired by the monologue. There isn't a set structure, but often there will be three scenes and then the monologist will come back on stage and either continue his or her original story, or begin a new monologue. The process repeats – if you are highly structured there should be three monologues and nine scenes – but often there is no set number of monologues or scenes.

The two forms are quite similar. The major difference is that in an Armando the monologist is a member of the team and often takes part in scenes, and more fully integrates his or her monologues into the performance, whereas with ASSSSCAT the monologist is often a guest and does not join in the improvisation.

Skills: Scene Development, Support Your Partner, Group Mind, Listening, Justification, Reincorporation, Agreement, Editing, Story-telling, and Making the Unexpected Choice.

Teaching Tips: When first starting it can be helpful to follow a more rigid structure. As you become more comfortable, allow yourself room to let additional scenes develop or insert more monologues or just generally play with the form. As with WeirDass, take an element from the story to springboard into a new scene instead of simply recreating the story. If you are using a guest monologist, be sure to do your best to make them look great.

Structure: Chain Smoking (or for a healthier alternative – Associative Scenes)

Description: 6–12 players. The concept is that you take something from the previous scene to inspire the next scene. So structurally it'll look a little bit like a Montage and a LaRonde going on a date. Ideally by "snatching" something from the previous scene, you keep the momentum of the form building without having to rely on plot or structure. You can use a character, line or phrase, gesture, sound, location, catchphrase, or prop to start the next scene. You can also use what's known as a "snatch edit." For instance, perhaps a character is writing with a pen – you can enter the scene and snatch the pen and begin a new scene by writing with the pen in a new scenario. You can also "stretch" the object and change it into something new. So perhaps you "snatch" the pen, but in your scene you transform it into a pool cue, or sword, or any other object. All that matters is that the transition is clear to the audience and your fellow players.

Skills: Scene Development, Support Your Partner, Group Mind, Listening, Justification, Reincorporation, Agreement, Editing, Storytelling, and Making the Unexpected Choice.

Teaching Tips: Try to find "unexpected" ways to link scenes together. Using a line of dialogue is fine, but be creative in the way that you link scenes. The audience will appreciate it and it will help build momentum. The danger in this form is cutting scenes too quickly and going on an associative run of quick scenes right out of the gate. You still want to take time to develop scenes.

Structure: The Living Room

Description: The form opens with the players forming a horseshoe at a "dinner party." They should take turns telling stories to one another based on the audience suggestion like you would at a dinner party. The stories should be true, or should be about events that

164

are actually happening in the world. Players can play characters, but should remain truthful and grounded. Eventually a player steps into the middle of the horseshoe and begins a scene inspired by the dinner party. As with all "inspired scenes," the scenes shouldn't just recreate the stories but should use them for inspiration. After a few scenes, the players should return to the dinner party, incorporating the scenic information into the conversation – don't just retell us what we just saw. Use the scenes for inspiration for new stories. Again, players then use the conversation for scenic inspiration and vice versa. As the form builds, the conversations should get shorter and shorter.

Skills: Scene Development, Support Your Partner, Group Mind, Listening, Justification, Reincorporation, Agreement, Editing, Storytelling, and Making the Unexpected Choice.

Teaching Tips: Again, the big thing is to not retell the stories or the scenes. You are using them as inspiration to see where they might take us, not to tell us where we've been.

Structure: The Movie

Description: The name pretty much sums it up: the ensemble works to improvise a movie. After getting an audience suggestion (it is popular to ask for a song lyric but not essential), the players begin narrating the opening, working to describe three separate scenes/characters/locations. Players often pick up descriptions mid-sentence. For instance:

165

> Player 1: "We open on a tracking shot of a lit-
>   tle boy playing baseball in his backyard.
>   He's wearing a Cubs hat and—"
> Player 2: "We see that his dad is on the porch
>   drinking a beer with no intention of play-
>   ing with his son."
> Player 3: "We see that the father has a large tat-
>   too poking out from underneath his ill-fitting
>   tank top. All we can see is O-U-G-H S-O-B."
> Player 4: "We cut away to a luxurious ocean
>   yacht. We pan across the ship and see the
>   captain, a tanned woman of about 35."
> Player 5: "She's wearing a white bikini with a
>   sheer sash tide around her waist, though it
>   does little to hide her amazing figure."

> Player 1: "The sun is blazingly bright and she
>   seems not to have a care in the world."
> Player 2: "Meanwhile in Des Moines there is a
>   farmer holding up an ear of corn. We can't
>   see his face behind the corn, but we can
>   tell something is wrong."

As each description emerges, another improviser steps on stage to become the characters that are mentioned. There is usually no dialogue; instead, the players mime what is being described. After the three scenes have been established, another improviser steps forward to give the title for the movie.

Player 1: "The camera cuts back to the little boy, who has just swung and missed, and the title appears across his face – 'Striking Out!' And we fade to the first scene."

From this point forward the improvisers would begin playing scenes from the movie, working with the given three scenes and adding new information as necessary. Improvisers not in scenes would continue to step forward to add stage directions, indicate lighting changes, camera movement angles, sound effects, and other cinematic elements. Players can use their hands to help isolate events – for instance, a player can step forward and frame out a character's eyes while saying "The camera pulls in tight for an extreme close up of Joe's eyes." Players on stage likewise work with the off-stage players to create camera effects – moving the action physically to the left or right for a pan, or totally reversing and having backs to the audience for a 180-degree pan, or by lying on the floor for an aerial shot.

It is also necessary to firmly establish a genre for the movie. Part of the fun of the structure is then satirizing and parodying the genre.

The movie ends when a player describes the moment before the closing credits, and states "The End appears on the screen."

Skills: Narrative, Character Development, Scene Painting, Scene Development, Group Mind, and Support Your Partner.

Teaching Tips: Focus less on the plot of the movie and more on the genre and characters. The audience will have a good time if the scenes are strong, the characters are compelling, and they recognize the genre. Like almost all long form, they are less interested with you creating a dynamic and miraculous plot.

Scene Painting is a technique that is at the heart of the movie. It can be used in any form or genre or scene, though like most tricks, it is best to use it sparingly. Essentially Scene Painting means that you are verbally describing what the audience is seeing in the environment. You aren't narrating the action; you are painting the scene. Usually a player will walk into the space and say, "We see a... " Or "There is a... ". You want to describe the environment, not dictate action for your fellow players. So saying, "There is an empty bag of potato chips. This makes Dale sad because he ate them all last night and he feels bad about it" is narrating action and not leaving "Dale" with much to do. A more effective version would be, "There is an empty bag of potato chips lying on the floor next to Dale's very worn recliner. The shades are drawn throughout the room, making it unnaturally dark. We see an old stain across the front of his shirt." This description tells us that Dale ate the chips and that he probably doesn't feel that great about himself, but it doesn't dictate the action. You are setting up an environment and situation for your fellow player to explore.

Structure: Go

Jeanne Leep showed this one to me at ATHE and I'm stealing it for you. The group begins by doing a word association. At any point an improviser can say "Go" after another player says their word and that player then has to deliver a short, true monologue that is based on the word just said (say Player 1 says "Banana" and Player 3 says "Go." Player 1 now gives a 30 second monologue about bananas in the context of the word association. In short, why did you say banana?). This word association-monologue opening can go on a bit longer than a traditional monologue opening. Players then transition and use the monologues as the basis for scenes.

Teaching Tips: This can be a gentle introduction to long form as there isn't really a structure to follow, and players are "forced" to give monologues. The big thing is honesty – make sure that the monologues are honest. You also want to make sure that the word association keeps a quick tempo.

The College Improv Team

A lot of you are already part of a group or team. Others of you are looking to join. Some of you might be starting a group. From the organizational structure, auditioning, rehearsing, performing, traveling, and even dating, there is a lot that goes into a successful college group, so here's some advice to help you navigate the waters.

One or Many

The first item to address is the makeup and structure of the group. There are two big options for college improv groups. The first is to form a single team (auditioned or open). The second, and the one I've found to be much more successful, is to create an umbrella organization that functions much like a professional theater. At the University of Missouri, for instance, Matt started MU Improv. Within MU Improv there are numerous smaller teams, much like there are many Harold teams at iO. Each team is self-formed, though an advisor/coach/president can make or tweak teams. Each team is in charge of its own content and style – whatever type of team you end up with, make sure that the team has a vision of what it wants to be that everybody agrees with.

The umbrella organization holds rehearsal at the same time, so all of the groups still see one another, but after whatever business you have to deal with and a short group warm-up/exercise, the individual teams go off on their own to rehearse. Multiple semi-autonomous teams gives them ownership of the group and helps expose the larger group to a number of styles. It also expands the membership, scope, and ultimately audience for the group. Each team or group has an individual leader or co-captain, who then reports to the organization's president and/or executive board. New members usually are grouped together and work with senior members of the group or a coach to teach them the ropes.

Either way, you need to have a clear leadership structure. This is especially true if your group doesn't have any faculty input or an outside coach/advisor. It can be tough to lead your peers, but having a set leadership structure makes it a lot easier. If it is clear that Emilio is the leader, then there will be less animosity, jealousy, and in-fighting when decisions need to be made. Each group is different, but here are some basic leadership positions to consider: a president/artistic director, a vice-president/vice-AD, a treasurer (because as you'll see, you are going to have money going in and out), and a secretary to keep notes of meetings and decisions and to schedule shows and reserve spaces. Just because you're in an improv group doesn't mean you shouldn't write things down. Take yourselves seriously.

To Audition or Not to Audition: That is the Question

Whatever structure your group takes, there is one big question: to audition or not. If you go down the one group route, and hopefully you have enough interest in your group that auditions are necessary, auditions are probably a good idea. If you only want one group, keeping the numbers low will help keep the quality high. An added side bonus is that it makes getting into the group a big deal, which can be a big deal for the group. Members who audition for a group and get in tend to take more ownership of the group. If you know that you can be cut because 40 other people auditioned for your spot, then you are a lot less likely to skip rehearsal and pull other crap that 18-year-olds do sometimes.

Improv auditions are tricky because the things that get you noticed in an audition tend to be the things that make you bad at improv. Standing out in an audition is great – standing out in an improv show is bad. Being funny in an audition is great – trying to be funny in improv is bad. While you can do a one-night audition, it's probably best to simply have your audition be a series of open rehearsals. This will allow you to more fully understand how people work and if they fit in the group because you will remove some of the immediate pressure from them. It'll also weed out folks who aren't interested in investing the time in a multi-week audition. If the number of folks auditioning makes having open rehearsals impossible, you should probably start thinking about an umbrella organization.

If you go down the umbrella organization route, then you really shouldn't audition. You should put restrictions on becoming a member,[1] but if somebody wants to improvise and they are willing to put in the time, then your group should give them a spot. That doesn't mean that every team (or individual) performs at every show, but we feel like it isn't up to us to tell you that you can't make shit up with us – playing is a right; performing is a privilege. Let us stress again that you do need membership requirements so that members take the group seriously. This usually isn't an issue for 90% of the members, but there will be a floating 10% that will come and go throughout the year. For an umbrella organization holding auditions within the group for a "travel team" is useful, so long as who is picking the team is clear. You certainly can pick one of your established teams, either through tacit consent, an in-house tournament, or vote. But you can also hold auditions for the special group that will represent the organization at outside events: tournaments, festivals, special performances, etc. This is where having a strong leadership structure and policy is helpful. If everyone knows how the team is picked (and who picks it), the less drama there will be.

Rehearsal

Remember earlier when we said you needed to rehearse? Well, that's still true. As a college group you should be rehearsing at minimum once a week for two hours. Twice a week is probably ideal at the college level depending on your show schedule. More than three times a week is asking a lot for full-time college students. You need to set a schedule. Rehearsals can't be on a rotating or need-to-know basis. They need to be every Tuesday night at 7pm. If you don't schedule rehearsal it'll be easy to move it around, and ultimately to skip rehearsal.

Rehearsal is where you build trust, learn skills, improve as individuals, build group mind, develop your style, build confidence, and did we say build trust? Yeah? Oh okay, so it's where you build trust. Because you need that trust to be successful together on stage. And that trust is built in rehearsal. It also helps set a professional tone for your group. It shows that you take improv seriously. Nobody else is going to take you or your group seriously until you do. So rehearse.

What should your rehearsals look like? Generally speaking, you want to do two contrasting warm-up exercises (something physical and energetic, and something that gets your improv brain tuned up and gets the group working together). From there, you should do one exercise to focus on a particular skill. If you do short form, then practice games (2–3) that emphasize that skill. If you do long form, do a few scenes and then practice your form once or twice, with particular emphasis on the "skill of the day."

As noted, rehearsals can take lots of forms, but here are some things that you should accomplish in rehearsal:

- You should be practicing skills. Even when you think you are great. Especially when you think you are great. Are you as good as TJ & Dave? Then keep working to get better. You should be focusing on skills at every rehearsal, but at least once a month you should spend an entire rehearsal working on skills. Build one skill at a time in these rehearsals. Focus on listening, then move on to physicality next month, then move on to editing. If you try to do everything all at once in one rehearsal, you tend not to get better. See Section III for ideas.

- You should be building group mind and camaraderie. The better you know each other – on stage and off – the better your improvisation will be. Remember the secret about basketball. Make sure at least one warm-up every rehearsal focuses at least partially on building group mind. Take five minutes to make plans to do something outside of rehearsal. You don't all have to be best friends, but think about the level of trust, camaraderie, and simply "being in on the joke" with groups of people that spend a lot of time together.

- You should be practicing structures or forms. Learn new ones. Practice old ones. Develop your own. It takes time and repetition to get good at a form, so put the time in. Pick one and get really good at it.

- You should be watching lots of improv. Watch pros, and watch each other in rehearsal. This is especially important if your college isn't near a city with professional improv. Watching others perform is one of the best ways to get better. It's a lot easier to tell what is making a scene work or what a scene is missing from the outside than it is from the inside, so take some time to watch. Seeing a Harold done by a professional team makes the form much easier to comprehend. And do it together. Go to shows together. Watch stuff online together. Listen to Jimmy Carrane's Improv Nerd podcasts together. Talk about it together.

- You should be simulating show experiences. With MU Improv and Albright Improv we do share time for the last half-hour of rehearsal. Each group/team gets ten minutes to perform for the group as though they were performing a show. Take the time to practice hosting and introducing groups and forms. Know if you want a back line or improvisers on the side. Get comfortable being on stage and being in front of an audience. Practice ending your sets. Practice your show polish. It can make a big difference in how your audience perceives your group.

You also should be thinking about a coach. This person is an outsider who will give you rehearsal and show notes, help structure rehearsal, and basically work to make you a better improv group. He or she will help you recognize and play to your strengths, as well as recognize and improve upon your weaknesses (both as individuals and as a team). A coach is different from a teacher and a director, though he or she will do some of both. A teacher brings in new exercises and works to teach skills while a coach works more to reinforce skills already taught. In simple terms, your rehearsal isn't a class so don't expect your coach to be your teacher. Generally a director works to create the show (and cast the show), whereas a coach is there to help you get better at a particular form or structure, like a Harold.

If you live in an area with lots of professional improv, hire someone to be your coach (yes, you should be paying your coach if they are a professional). Go to local theaters, go to shows, and ask. If you have a faculty member with improv experience, invite them to be your coach – even if only for a short time. If you have no faculty members with improv experience, invite an acting professor to a rehearsal or two. Make it clear that you are only asking them for one or two nights. They are more than likely already very, very, very busy, so asking for one rehearsal increases the likelihood of them saying yes. Give them something specific to look for in rehearsal, for instance, "We are working on developing strong wants in our scenes, and we just wanted an outside eye to help." They can give you basic acting and staging notes, and hopefully they'll see the commitment and professionalism of your group, which can only help your place on the food chain. Some faculty really have no idea what you are doing, especially in rehearsal, so letting them in (if only briefly) can help them understand what it is you are doing and help them advocate for you. Believe it or not, most faculty actually want their students to succeed.

If you have no outside input, it is possible to internally coach. If you go down this route, designate one member coach for a set period (anywhere from one rehearsal to a month). This person no longer participates in exercises or shows. He or she needs to step out of the performance arena so as to remain objective. It can be difficult to give your peers notes, so be sure to firmly establish a coaching structure. Everyone should know that Rob is coach for October, for instance, and everyone needs to agree to the situation beforehand. As coach, keep your notes professional, objective, and to the point. This isn't your opportunity to wax poetic about your improv philosophy or to take out your frustration on Logan. Be professional.

You should give everyone in the group (within reason) a chance to coach over the course of the semester or year, with more experienced players coaching first (and probably for longer periods of time). If only one or two players act as coach, it can lead to some animosity, mainly in the form of "Why does Joe get to be coach but I don't?" Obviously different members of the group will have varying levels of success as coach, but it is important to allow everyone a voice. Remember, if you know your group can't handle self-coaching from a personality/team chemistry standpoint, don't self-coach. It is a really tricky thing and can cause more trouble than it's worth.

174

Putting on a Show

Now that you've made it this far, let's briefly talk about putting on a show. Some of these things are obvious and self-explanatory, and some of them have been learned the hard way. Either way, this section is designed to help you put together an effective show.

Big Picture Planning

When To Perform

This depends a lot on the size of school/audience, and the obligations of the members. Ideally you'll perform every week. If you are an umbrella organization this doesn't require every member to perform every week – usually every team will get on stage at least once a month, if not more. At a small school like Albright where most of our improvisers are in mainstage shows, sing in the choirs, and play for the bands, we aim for 2–4 weeks between shows. At Mizzou and Illinois State, we performed every week. So find a balance that works for you. If you find yourself in the position to schedule a show, here are some things to keep in mind:

1. Do your best to set some kind of regular schedule, whether every Tuesday night, or the first Friday of the month. Make it as easy as possible for your audience. If your school has someone who schedules space or runs the campus calendar, do your best to get your info in early so that you can be "established."
2. What else is happening on campus? Especially in the performing arts. Remember that both your performers and audience members are heavily involved, so look for a date(s) that is as open as possible ... and yes, this might mean a weeknight. This applies to both one-off shows and regular scheduling. If there are music concerts on Thursdays, then maybe you don't want to have improv shows on Thursdays.
3. Where are you performing? There are usually several places on campus to perform. The mainstage theater actually probably isn't the best place. You want somewhere small and cramped where audiences are forced to be close together. Laughter is contagious and communal – help the process along.
4. How can you tie your show to some other event taking place? For instance, Albright Improv usually performs a show on Friday nights after mainstage productions, which helps build

175

audience. What else is happening on campus that can inspire a show (and build audience)?

Where to Perform

What to look for in a venue, either on campus or off campus:

1. Suitability: Is this a good space for improv? As noted above, generally you want to find a more intimate setting than a traditional theater (for reference, most improv theaters are small and feel a lot like a bar... and make a lot of their money from said bar). Improv is a communal thing, so a space that is a bit confined is actually a good thing. And people tend to laugh if other people are laughing. And other people tend to laugh when they feel like part of a group.
2. Availability: Is the space available? Sometimes you have to decide between a particular date and a particular venue.
3. Accessibility: This is less of an issue on campus, but do people know where the space is and how to get there (and off campus the all-important question is: Where can I park?). Also, is the space accessible for folks in wheelchairs or with other impairments? Hopefully your campus is an accessible campus, but if it isn't do your part to make it one.
4. Schedule your venues as early as possible. Schedules fill up and spaces get taken really quickly on college campuses. If you find a space you really like, do whatever you can to make that your home and work to schedule it on an ongoing basis.

Who Performs?

This can be one of the trickier parts of running a college improv group, especially since most of the members are probably going to be your friends. So it is paramount to make clear rules or guidelines for who gets to perform. It helps to instill a mantra like "playing is a right; performing is a privilege." If you have multiple teams, make it clear what the criteria for performing actually are – is it a rotating schedule? Do the senior teams get to pick dates? Does the E-Board pick? Whatever method you choose, make sure that it is clear and everybody knows the criteria. In terms of individual members, again the most important thing is clear and consistent guidelines. For instance, if you miss a rehearsal, can you still perform? How many can you miss? When can you miss them? When do new members get to perform? Do they have to train for a semester, or do they go right on stage? Have a policy, make it known to everyone right from the start, and then stick to it.

Advertising

If you haven't noticed, there are eight bajillion things happening on campus at the same time, so people aren't just going to magically appear at your improv show. Having a regular show schedule and "home" venue helps, as does tying your show into other events on campus. Make someone in charge of advertising and public relations. Don't make this a secret. Make it an in-writing position. If you want people at the show, then it is your job to get them there! Advertising can take many forms; here are a few of the things that folks typically do:

- Posters – Posters are typically designed two weeks prior to performance, and are printed and posted one week prior to performance. Posting too early can cause the event to seem old hat and students will often forget about it. Typically posters are 12x18 and are ideally allocated for in the year's budget. If you have a regular performance slot (e.g. Tuesdays at 9pm), rotate new posters in every few weeks.
- Social media – Use social media to create events, solicit suggestions, post pictures and news, make videos, and generally drum up buzz. Create a website, YouTube channel, and Twitter/Facebook/Instagram/Whatever is Popular Now. Post stuff on there people will want to interact with.
- Word of mouth – As much as posters and social media work, nothing gets people to a show more than word of mouth. And word of mouth starts with each and every member of the group. Word of mouth means that you need to tell people that you are in a show. It also means that you need to be professional on stage and deliver a solid product so that audience members say nice things to one another (and their friends) about the show. For all the "regulars" at your show, remember that there is probably someone there for the first time. Make his experience great.
- Campus media – There are several media outlets on campus that can help publicize a show, or the group as a whole. Making contact with these outlets can help spread the word

177

around campus. Remember, they are looking for content so don't think of yourself as pushing things onto them ... think of it as though you are helping them out with a story about this great improv group.

- Local media – There are also a few local media outlets that are worth looking into. While most of your audience will be campus based, it never hurts to have non-campus-based media. A clip or story in a non-school paper, for instance, can be very helpful for festival applications, grants, etc.

178

The Show Itself

You've set up a performance, you've advertised the hell out of it, and now you've got a room full of people. What now? Let's back up a bit. Setting up a show properly can go a long way toward the overall success of the performance.

Show Order

The first step to a successful show is a great show order. Whether it is short form, long form, or sketch, the order sets up the audience. Variety of games, styles, and players is key. For short form especially, make sure to balance the show. This means the types of games, the number of players per game, the actual players in games, the length of games, and the style of comedy. For instance, people get bored if you have a show with three guessing games. For long form, think about the order of teams, or if you have one team doing multiple forms, how you order the forms. You want your show to have a forward momentum – so help yourself by properly scheduling it.

Casting

Once you have a show order, if you are doing short form you need to cast it. In many ways this will be the hardest aspect of planning the show, especially with a large group. There are several methods to cast:

- The team leader(s) cast games.

    This puts a lot of pressure on team leader(s), but is probably the most efficient way to cast. Team members can express a game preference beforehand, but the team leader has the final say. Inevitably, someone will be mad.
- Each member can select one game they'd like to play. Everybody gets one choice and then we move on to second choices.

    This is the most democratic way to cast. Everybody theoretically gets to play one game they really want to play. However, that doesn't mean that they should be playing said game. Inevitably, someone will be mad.
- Games are announced and the first people to volunteer get to play (they then cannot volunteer again until others have been cast).

    This method favors the vocal and can leave more introverted members taking the leftovers. Inevitably, someone will be mad.

- With long form, there really isn't casting. If you have multiple teams performing, generally the more experienced team closes the show. Either that, or simply rotate the order from show to show so each team gets to open, close, or fill in the middle at some point.
- With sketch, the director assigns roles and orders the sketches.

Hosting

For short form you can have one main host and then a host for each game, or just one main host who does everything. There isn't really a set rule, so one person could do all the hosting, or you can break it up however you'd like. For long form usually one person takes on hosting duties since there isn't quite as much to do. The only thing that really matters is that the host clearly and efficiently executes his or her duties. The host should do the following:

- Set up the game or structure. Tell us what the game/structure is, and the basic info we need to understand what is about to happen. In other words, know the rules. Don't teach us the games, just give us what we need to understand what is about to happen.
- Solicit any audience suggestions (see below for more info).
- Recap any audience suggestions.
- End the game. Generally if there isn't an ending built into the game, the host cuts the game at the appropriate time.
- Additionally, the host needs to maintain a welcoming persona. In a lot of ways the host is saying to the audience, "It's okay to laugh at this." So it probably isn't a good idea to yell at them or antagonize them.

Sample long form host: "Hi! We're Soviet Purgatory and tonight we are going to be performing a Harold for you. The Harold is a long form structure that features three unrelated scenes that repeat in some way three times and all magically comes together in the end. Can we have a suggestion to start?" At the end of the show, the host then closes the show. "Thank you for being a great audience. We're Soviet Purgatory. Check us out online at albrightimprov.com, and be sure to come back next week!"

Sample short form host for Party Quirks (we're assuming the show has already been introduced): "Hello! The next game we are going to play for you is Party Quirks. For this game, Jon (or whoever the player is) is hosting a party, but the guests all have a quirk that he must guess. So somebody take Jon away for a moment (another player takes Jon out of the playing space to somewhere he can't hear). Okay, I need a physical quirk for Theresa? (Gets suggestion). She's got two right feet. Great. Now for Andy, I need an emotional state. (Gets suggestion). Nice! He takes everything ultra-personally. Finally, for Rebecca I need a tick. (Gets suggestion). She touches her nose every time someone uses the word "potato." Quick recap, Theresa (she states her quirk), Andy (states his quirk), and Rebecca (states her quirk). Great! Oh, Johnny Boy! Come start the party!"

Soliciting Audience Suggestions

Getting suggestions from the audience is one of the host's main jobs. Some games or structures have a specific need, such as, "What crime did this person commit?", while other games or structures are a bit more open-ended, for instance, "We need a suggestion to start our Harold." Some tips for soliciting suggestions:

- Ask a particular chunk of the crowd, rather than everyone. "From the first two rows I need a reason you'd betray your best friend." This helps focus the suggestion and avoids confusion and mass yelling/chaos. Be sure to rotate sections so you aren't always asking the same people.
- Let the players make the characters/relationship/situation specific. When you are asking for a relationship, all you need is "Sisters." You don't need, "Sisters who are really lovers and the one sister wants to kill the other sister because she slept with her husband, who likes whales but not all whales, only gay whales. Condom." Remember that audience suggestions are jumping-off points and not what the scene must be about.
- Sometimes asking a really specific question can actually lead to a broader answer. For instance, "Who is your favorite family member to sit next to at Thanksgiving?" is a nice alternative to "Can I have a relationship?" The person will then say, "My sister." Now you have a relationship.
- Don't feel like you must take the first thing you hear. At the same time, don't drag it out forever. Inevitably on a college campus the first thing you are going to hear will be some allusion to

181

pornography or sexual acts. While that works sometimes, it's probably best if every game isn't based on "Cat porn."

- Establish a rapport with the audience. They want to be a part of the action, so you need to make them feel that way while still maintaining your authority as host.

Show Polish

Now that you have the games/structures and the folks playing, the next bit is to pay attention to show polish. This means that the host(s) and players know the rules of the game, the show order (and where they fit), and take the performance seriously.

- Many times performers ask to be cast in a game or structure they have never played. Sorry, but we rehearse for a reason.
- Laughing on stage is a sign that you are not fully invested in the scene. It's a cheap ploy to draw attention to yourself at the expense of your partners and the scene itself. So cut it out. It signals that you are not invested, you are selfish, you are not prepared, and that you were not expecting you or your scene partner to do anything humorous. Your character can certainly laugh, but you as an actor should not.
- When you aren't on stage, shut up and pay the fuck attention. Don't talk and don't distract the audience. If you are a member of the group and the show isn't even worthy of your attention, why should the audience pay attention?
- Put on some fucking pants and a nice shirt. No graphic tees. No dresses. No shorts. Take off your hat. Pull back your hair. You don't need gobs of makeup. Wear flat shoes. Take out your neon scrunchies. Look nicer than the audience. You don't need to be in formal wear, but you need to look presentable. If you look nice the audience will give you more status. If you look like a slob you have lowered their expectations and overall impression of you. Sloppy teams have to work twice as hard to win over an audience as a well-put-together team. Appearances matter.
- Respect the stage. Respect the performance. Respect your audience. Playing in rehearsal is a right; performing is a privilege. Treat it as such every time you take the stage.

182

Post Show

After the show it is recommended that players do some sort of assessment. It can be formalized, or simply players chatting about what happened. You don't need to dwell on things, but talk about what worked, and what you'd like to accomplish with the next show – this should take less than ten minutes. This is not a bitch session or a call-everyone-out session. If you have a coach, let them lead notes. If you don't have a coach and you have access to an outsider, let the outsider lead notes. It can be tough for peers to give and take notes from one another. It is certainly possible, but it takes a certain level of trust, self-confidence, and intelligence. If you don't have a coach or outsider, having each player answer these three simple questions is a good start: What's one thing you did that you liked? What's one thing that somebody else did that you liked? And what's one thing you want to work on for the next show? These questions keep things positive (often the hardest question to answer is the first as beginning improvisers are quick to beat themselves up), make comments about other players complimentary, and force players to think actively about critiques rather than negatively.

183

Dating and Fighting

It happens. Let's face it, you are spending a lot of time together. You both have at least one similar interest. You probably think the other is talented and funny. You love the way this person supports you and challenges you. She makes you laugh. He makes you smile. You're 20 and she's 20 and you're both quirkily good looking and funny and you spend most of the day together – so you're probably going to start dating. Are we going to tell you not to date? Of course not. I met my wife in an improv group. Though if your entire group is made up of couples, you are courting disaster. Here's some improv dating advice won through some relationship scars.

Guide to Improv Dating

Do keep in mind that you are going to see this person all the time. He or she will be at rehearsal. He or she will be at the shows. So know going into it that you are going to see each other all the time. That doesn't mean don't give it a romantic whirl, but it means that if it doesn't work out it'll be a trickier situation because you can't just cut that person out of your life. And most of your friends are going to be involved at some level. It also means that you need to pick – you are either dating or you aren't.

Don't have a one-night stand with someone in your group. You *will* see them. And somebody in your group will probably do a scene about a one-night stand, and you'll feel really awkward, then everyone will figure it out, and then it'll be even more awkward. Plus, just on principle it isn't the nicest thing to do to people.

Do leave your baggage – both good and bad – at the door. Make a clear and defined line between your improv relationship and your romantic relationship. You are both members of an equal ensemble. If you are dating, chances are that you two know each other pretty darn well, and have inside jokes. That stuff needs to stay out of the room. Draw a line between your personal life and your business life (improv).

Don't take scenes personally. They are not a reflection of your relationship in any way. If your boyfriend breaks up with you on stage, it isn't real (or he's just a giant dick so you should probably break up anyway). If your girlfriend is in a flirtatious scene with another guy, she isn't cheating on you. If he cuts your scene it doesn't mean he doesn't love you … or like you a lot … or wherever you are in your relationship.

Do tell each other how funny and talented you both are.

Don't give each other notes. If you are in a healthy relationship, you should be able to be honest with each other. But you know what, don't do it. You might have a great insight about your boyfriend's scene, but don't tell him. Don't open Pandora's Box. You two should feel free to talk about improv, and celebrate all of the wonderful things you are each doing, but stay away from the "constructive" note.

Do feel free to flirt (if you aren't dating another member of the group … or anyone else).

Don't do this:

"I'm Joe. I've been flirting with Michelle for weeks. I think she's pretty great. We went out for milkshakes the other day. Last night, I slept with Jody, who is also in improv. Now Michelle is all upset. I didn't do nothing wrong."

Do realize that you are probably going to be annoying and cutesy when you first start dating (or forever).

Don't consciously do annoying and cutesy things in rehearsal – no pet names, weird touching, or sensual back-rubs. Keep the giggling to a minimum. And please don't use shows or rehearsals to "test your boyfriend/girlfriend."

185

Guide to Improv Breakups

It happens. You tried to "Yes, And" your relationship but the scene ultimately needed to be cut. Here are some ways you can make it less terrible on you and your group.

Do continue to support one another in scenes.

Don't criticize one another outside of rehearsal (or during rehearsal). Vent to your non-improv friends. If you don't have any non-improv friends, make some. It'll be healthier for you regardless of your romantic life, it will give you more material for scenes, and it'll mean you have people that'll come to your shows.

Do tell members of the ensemble about it.

Don't tell them all at once at the beginning of rehearsal.

Do come to rehearsal with a positive attitude.

Don't drag everyone into your personal love abyss.

Do continue to be an equal member of the ensemble.

Don't make your friends pick sides when it comes to improv. If Sally does a scene with Estefan, she isn't betraying you. And *don't* pull rank. If you have been in the group for three years and your ex joined this semester, that doesn't mean he or she has to quit and you get to stay.

Do continue to participate as fully as before the breakup.

Don't seek out scenes or games with your ex. If it happens, it happens. But don't force it to happen. It'll be awkward for everyone.

Don't flaunt how well you are doing, or how easy the breakup was for you.

Don't start dating another improviser in the group for at least six months.

What About That Guy?

Dating can bring about all sorts of joy and strife for improv teams. But even teams that don't kiss each other can have problems. At some point in your college improv life (and beyond), you are going to come across "that guy." That Guy is different for everybody, but basically it will come out like this – "I really love our group, but That Guy is making it tough." "Our shows are good, but That Guy keeps going for cheap jokes." "I really want to tell That Guy he's ruining our group." "That Guy is a stage hog." "That Guy doesn't get the rules." "That Guy keeps pandering and mugging for the audience." "That Guy doesn't take any of our suggestions." "That Guy thinks he's better than us." And whatever other version it might be, there's one person that seems to be out of step with the group... or there's simply somebody you don't like.

The problem can be magnified by the fact that your improv options might be limited at your school, and/or you all hang out together constantly in your little college fishbowl of a bubble. That Guy might be your best friend, or roommate, or significant other... or somebody you don't really like (or maybe That Guy is you). So what should you do?

First of all, remember to play along, especially during a performance. If That Guy is mugging to the audience, or denying your offers, or making you the stupid guy that loves elephant dick, then play along. It isn't going to do you any good to try and correct him in front of an audience. In fact, it's probably going to make *you* look like an asshole. Remember basic improv rules: agree and play along. If he is making you uncomfortable on stage because he's being a real-life asshole, or making you do some weird sexualized character, then call him on it or step out of the scene. But if he or she is just being an improv dick, your best course of action is to play along.

If you have a coach, you can talk to your coach about it. Let your coach tell That Guy to cut back on his walk-ons, or to realize that he doesn't need to be in every scene, or that he's ignoring relationships in scenes and going straight to Wacky Town, USA. That's kind of the coach's job.

You can also talk to That Guy. When you do talk to him, don't attack him. Make sure to use specific examples about the group. "When we go for crazy right at the top of scenes it really doesn't seem to work." Then give a specific example. "Like the time you started a scene as the masturbating crab who is also an insult comic dying from stomach cancer." Then offer up another example of a time that the team held off on the crazy. "I feel like the scene where we were breaking up at the zoo was a really grounded and funny scene." Somebody will undoubtedly bring up an example of a crazy scene that worked. Don't worry about it. You aren't here to police. This isn't a bitch session. This isn't a note session tailored for That Guy.

You'll probably want to talk to another player about That Guy. If it makes you feel better, then do it – for 30 seconds. But don't gang up as a team on That Guy, because that'll just end up being counterproductive ... which is why you want to give specific examples about the team and not generalization about That Guy.

The best course of action? Think about the type of group you want and the type of energy you like. Then bring that energy, focus, and point of view with you to rehearsals and shows. Focusing on negativity and constantly being frustrated will come through in your work and attitude. Don't let the critic take over. Make the active choice and bring solid positive energy. If you don't, chances are you're going to become That Guy.

A Note About Diversity

Improv has historically been dominated by white, liberal, heterosexual men. A lot of improv still features white, liberal, heterosexual men. And a lot of improvisers like to fall back on stereotypes when playing another race, gender, or sexual orientation (or when playing with someone from another race, gender, or sexual orientation). It's easy to play stereotypes. You'll usually get a pretty easy laugh. But it's not only usually offensive – it's bad comedy. Improv is about being honest and truthful and stereotypes are rarely honest or truthful. People of other races, genders, and sexual orientations aren't only black/female/gay – they are people. And in scenes they are characters that want things, that have emotions, that do a million things that have nothing to do with race/gender/sexual orientation. In case you didn't know ...

The African-American guy in your group knows that he's black. You don't have to point it out in every scene. You also don't need to make him a criminal, gangsta, or any other stereotype you can think of.

The women in your group aren't there to be the wives and girl-friends in every scene. They aren't there to be won as sexual trophies in scenes.

If someone is gay they aren't overly flamboyant and sassy. There have already been enough scenes for all of our lifetimes between two straight guys where one pretends to be gay and all the jokes are about gay sex – we don't need yours. Not all lesbians are butch.

Here's a helpful fill-in-the-blank for you:

Not all _____ (insert any race, ethnicity, gender you like) are _____ (insert stereotype here). Treat them like actual people.

Some Other Ideas About Your Group

- Become a recognized organization on campus. This will give you access to money. Access to money is very helpful for some of your ideas. Plus if you are getting money, the faculty and administration will take your group more seriously.
- No matter where you are located, go see improv. Preferably see it live, but if you can't, there is a ton of stuff online now. Seeing professionals can make the learning curve a lot shorter. Watch together.
- Go to an improv festival just to watch… and talk improv with folks that have been doing this a lot longer than you.
- Try to perform at an improv festival.
- Make friends with other area colleges and perform with each other and at each other's schools. Performing in front of new audiences is great practice, and will keep you from falling back on what you think "your audience wants." Performing in front of other improvisers pushes you to up your game… plus you can steal forms from each other.
- Bring in professional improvisers to teach a workshop or do a show. Most improvisers are very generous about helping younger improvisers. It's great to hear an outside voice and get a new perspective. They will teach you things you don't know. They will show you things you don't know. You will be a better improviser the next day. It's also cool to literally pay it forward. There isn't a lot of money in improv, so if you've got some (because you

are a recognized student organization), pay people that are really good at improv. Hosting professional shows can also help build and expand your local audience and help you gain recognition on campus and with the administration. Not sure where to find a professional group? Well, let's take a look.

Note

1 For example, new members must be on a training group for a semester (only rehearsal, no shows); they must attend a set number of rehearsals; they must read certain books; or meet any set requirements you deem fitting for your group. Make the requirements clear and consistent.

189

A Guide To Professional Training

There are tons of professional improv theaters across the country, with more and more popping up every year. Almost all of them offer some kind of training. Whether you are aspiring to become a professional improviser, want to take improv classes to further your on-camera career, will take improv into the business world, or simply want to meet new people, classes are a great way to learn about the community and get involved. Almost all theaters cast their teams and shows from students who have taken classes, so if you want to do improv at iO, for instance, you need to take their classes first. Most classes are broken up into levels. Each level is generally about eight weeks long, with one two to four-hour class per week.

These classes aren't free – as of this printing, classes range from about $200–$500 per level, so we thought we'd give you a little primer to help you decide where you might start. Some schools offer internships for students to help defray costs, and most schools do offer students free admission to shows (or at least a discount), so taking classes is also a great way to see a lot of improv. While they can be expensive, most students find that the benefits ultimately far outweigh the costs. Speaking of shows, it is a good idea to attend shows at the theaters before taking classes. Being at a show will tell you a lot about the theater's style, performers, and atmosphere (as well as giving you a sneak peek at your future teachers). Seeing shows is a great way to get a feel for the theater and where you might fit – think of it as though you are going on college visits again – only this time without mom and dad.

This section isn't meant as a Princeton Review-style ranking, but rather as a collection of some of the top improv schools and what they offer. We have given an overview of the improv classes in Chicago, New York, and Los Angeles, as well as a handful of the best known schools outside of those cities. We've done our best to describe their curriculums, though we haven't provided a thorough critical examination – our goal isn't to rank the schools. This isn't an exhaustive list of every improv class in the country – new theaters and schools are popping up seemingly every day – but it should give you a good idea about what is available to you.

191

Chicago

Chicago is the hub of improvisation. Contemporary improvisation started in Chicago, and many of the leading improv theaters call Chicago home. You don't have to live in Chicago to do improv, as you'll see (and as you know since we'll just assume that not all of you go to school in Chicago), but it is "the promised land."

iO

The home of the Harold, iO teaches a relationship-based style of improvisation based on the work of Del Close and Charna Halpern and found in *Truth in Comedy*. Students learn the fundamentals of scene building, with the Harold forming the bedrock of the training curriculum. The "support your partner" ethos preached in class leads students to often comment about the sense of community and the tightknit nature of the theater. Featuring some of the best teachers in improvisation, iO is widely regarded as one of the top improv schools in the world.

The improv curriculum features five levels (with a 4 and 4B, and 5 and 5B).

Level 1 teaches the basics of iO's style of improvisation.
Level 2 focuses on creating characters, group mind, and object/ environment work.
Level 3 is all about two-person scenes.
Level 4 teaches students how to perform the Harold.
Level 4B explores other long form structures.
Level 5 is the advanced Harold level where students really work on executing the Harold as an ensemble.
Level 5B requires students to create an original long form show, which will receive a short run at iO.

After "graduation" students are eligible to be placed on House teams that perform Harolds. Not all students are placed on teams.

iO also offers a writing program that focuses on creating material for sitcoms, late-night television, and *Saturday Night Live*. There are also electives for musical improv and creating solo material.

The Second City

With classes in Chicago, Hollywood, and Toronto, The Second City is the largest school of improvisation in the world. Located in the bustling

Pipers Alley, with a variety of stages and classrooms, and students and performers constantly shuttling about, Second City can feel a bit like a university union. They offer classes in improv, writing, acting, music, physical theater, film and television, directing, as well as a variety of special topics. In conjunction with Columbia College in Chicago, they also offer an off-campus study semester called Comedy Studies.

The improv training program is based on the teachings of Viola Spolin and features levels A through E.

Improvisation A focuses on the basic building blocks of scenic improvisation.
Improvisation B moves forward to focus on improvising scenes.
Improvisation C is an introduction to character work.
Improvisation D is an advanced scene and character work class.
Improvisation E is all about improvisation in performance.
*Class performances are held at the end of the C, D, and E levels.

There are several options for students in addition to the A–E sequence, including the Improv for Actors sequence (for those folks who prefer scripted acting but still want to arm themselves with improv techniques), Scenic Improv 1 and 2, Solo Performance, Long Form Improv, and more. There are also teen and youth classes, classes for autism spectrum disorder students, classes for educators, and more.

After the A–E sequence, students are eligible to audition for the Conservatory (any student who has completed one year of professional improv training – not necessarily at Second City – and one post-high school acting class is eligible, so many students opt to take classes at iO or The Annoyance first and then directly audition for the Conservatory). The Conservatory trains students in the Second City method of using improv to create satirical sketch revues. The Conservatory has six levels:

Level 1 is advanced improvisational scene work.
Level 2 focuses on personal characters and the improviser as the actor.
Level 3 is about acting and character. *Note: Students must re-audition for Level 3 to continue in the program.
Level 4 is about style and forms.
Level 5 focuses on generating satirical material.
Level 6 is where students get to create and perform an original revue.

193

As noted above, in addition to the improvisation classes listed, there are numerous other courses offered, including a six-level Comedy Writing program that teaches the foundations of sketch comedy and culminates in writing a Second City-style revue.

The Annoyance

The third major school of improvisation in Chicago is at The Annoyance Theatre. Whereas iO classes are built around the Harold and Second City classes ultimately are structured around sketch revues, The Annoyance is focused on the individual improviser rather than any particular rules or structures – read *Improvise: Scene From the Inside Out*. There are six levels of classes at The Annoyance.

> AP1 – Ultimate Beginner Improv is a survey course in improvisation. It covers various forms and genres and is aimed at folks with little improv experience.
>
> AP2 – Annoyance Philosophy, Scene Initiation, and POV. This level focuses on personal responsibility in a scene; in short it introduces The Annoyance's belief that your prime responsibility is to take care of yourself in a scene. *Note – students with a strong improv background or who have completed training at iO or Second City can start at this level with approval.
>
> AP3 – Exploring the Elements; Patterns in Scenes – This level explores character, environment, and status with an eye toward creating patterns and games in scenes.
>
> AP4 – The Scene as a Whole – In this level students work on developing strong scenes.
>
> AP5 – Variety, Specificity, and More Complex Scenes – This level is all about making strong and specific choices to move your improv to the next level.

The Annoyance also offers a two-part Writing Program that ends in a performance of a newly written show.

pH Comedy Theater

pH training focuses on performance and stage time. Every week students meet for a particular lesson, and then head out on stage on Thursday night to perform. The program is audition based, and students are put together into teams that then stay together throughout the training process. The entire training program consists of four levels, and at the end of training student teams can audition to become a pH House Team. There is also a two-level musical improv program.

Chemically Imbalanced Comedy

While CIC doesn't currently offer ongoing classes, they do hold a College Bootcamp in the summer. The two-week intensive meets for five hours, five days a week and is designed specifically for college improvisers. Week 1 focuses on building and reinforcing basic skills necessary for scene work, while Week 2 focuses on ensemble play. Many teachers at CIC either teach, perform, or have trained at iO, Second City, and/or The Annoyance.

New York

Improv is a relative newcomer to New York City, which has a long and storied stand-up comedy tradition. Nevertheless, it has become one of the leading improv cities in the world thanks in large part to the success of the Upright Citizens Brigade and its alums.

Upright Citizens Brigade

The UCB Training Center is the only accredited improv and sketch comedy school in the country. They offer courses in improv and sketch comedy, as well as an application-only advanced study program that prepares students for a life in professional comedy. UCB classes are notorious for selling out quickly, in less than a minute after they are posted, so you might have to be diligent to get in the door. Much like Second City in Chicago, UCB is the largest school in NYC, and because of its reputation there tends to be a more competitive vibe amongst some students. Instructors do their best to combat this mindset and most classes have a strong communal sense. Prep yourself by reading *The Upright Citizens Brigade Comedy Improvisation Manual*.

The improv program features four levels.

Improv 101: Improv Basics teaches the basics of how to perform long form improv.

Improv 201: The Game of the Scene introduces UCB's guiding principle – the game of the scene.

Improv 301: Harold Structure focuses on the Harold. Unlike iO, however, UCB's Harold focuses on the game of the scene.

Improv 401: Harold Workshop is a more advanced and intense study of the Harold.

After Improv 401 students are eligible to apply for the Advanced Study program.

There is also a three-level sketch program that begins with sketch basics, moves on to collaboration and pitching, and culminates in writing a sketch show that will be staged at UCB.

The Peoples Improv Theater (The PIT)

The PIT offers a wide array of courses in improv, sketch comedy, solo performance, and a highly acclaimed professional writing program.

The PIT offers a six-level improv curriculum, with a class performance after levels 1–5.

Level 0: The Joy of Improv is for those with little improv background.
Level 1: Intro to Improv explores the fundamentals of improvisation.
Level 2: Scenework is exactly what it sounds like – it's all about scene work.
Level 3: Intro to Longform focuses on the basic skills necessary for success in long form improv while not specifically teaching to one particular form.
Level 4: Advanced Longform builds on Level 3 by further exploring long form techniques.
Level 5: Improv Performance Study requires students to create and perform an original long form structure.

The PIT also offers a three-level Sketch Writing Program, as well as a Professional Writing Program with classes on Writing for Late Night TV, Sitcom Writing, The Late Night Writers' Room, and Writing for SNL.

The Magnet Theater

Like its NYC counterparts, The Magnet offers classes in improvisation, musical improv, sketch comedy, writing, and storytelling. They also host drop-in workshops where students can show up at a particular time and work with a Magnet instructor or team. Much like The PIT, The Magnet has a very homey feel to its classes, with students often commenting about the sense of community that can be found at the theater.

The Magnet Training Center offers a six-level improv program.

Level 1: The Principles of Improv is the Magnet's introductory class focusing on improv basics.
Level 2: Intro to Long Form uses the skills from Level 1 to create long form improv.
Level 3: Long Form Intensive focuses exclusively on the Harold.
Level 4: Senior Project requires students to more fully explore another long form structure, culminating in a four-week run.
Level 5: Improv Revue is the first level in the Improv Conservatory, and focuses again on a specific long form structure that the students then perform in a four-week run.

Level 6: Team Performance Workshop, with instructor approval, focuses on creating a strong and dynamic ensemble, which will then complete an eight-week run of shows. At the end of the class students are eligible to audition for membership on a Megawatt Team.

Chicago City Limits

Unlike the other three NYC schools, Chicago City Limits doesn't solely teach long form techniques but instead focuses simply on creating scenes. Featuring a robust program for non-improvisers, business professionals, and teens, CCL also offers a three-level curriculum that emphasizes scenic building blocks, narrative techniques, and improvised musical skills.

198

Los Angeles

The center of the film universe is also home to some of the country's best improv. Because of improv's prevalence in film and commercials, there are plenty of schools to choose from to hone your chops while waiting for your big break.

The Groundlings

The Groundlings School is one of LA's oldest, and offers classes for professionals, teens, and those new to improvisation. Students graduate from the school into the Sunday Company, before being invited into the Main Company.

Students must audition for the Core Track, which has three levels and then an Upper Division Performance Track.

BASIC teaches the fundamentals of improv through exercises and theater games. *At the end of the class students meet with their teacher who will then recommend if the student should move on to INTERMEDIATE, repeat BASIC, or be dismissed from the Core Track.

INTERMEDIATE focuses on character work, scene work, and developing monologues. *Again, the instructor recommends advancement, repetition, or dismissal.

ADVANCED focuses further on character development while also exploring different improv styles and techniques. The ADVANCED class culminates in an improv show on the student stage.

Select students are then invited into the Upper Division – Performance Track, which consists of two additional classes.

LAB I: Writing Lab focuses on developing scripted scenes and monologues to be performed in a showcase.

LAB II: Advanced Lab serves as an "improv group" to develop material for two performances (one halfway through the course and another at the end).

Students who have completed the above courses are then eligible to be invited to join the Sunday Company. Not all students are invited to join. The Sunday Company writes and performs a new sketch and improv show every week, coincidentally on Sunday. Select Sunday Company members are then invited to join the Main Company.

199

iO West

Using the same philosophy as its older sibling in Chicago, iO West's training is based on Del Close and Charna Halpern's teachings and rooted in the Harold. The improv curriculum is slightly different to Chicago, and there is a more expansive writing program aimed at television. iO West also offers a five-week Summer Intensive that is particularly appealing for college students.

The improv curriculum features seven levels.

Level 1 – Introduction to Improv

Level 2 – Character & Game focuses on creating characters and finding games in scenes.

Level 3 – Intro to Harold provides a basic entry into the world of Harold.

Level 4 – Advanced Scene Work focuses on techniques to improve scene work.

Level 5 – Harold builds on the previous two levels, and features four performances on the iO stages.

Level 6 – Advanced Harold requires students to perform Harolds that do not follow the traditional "training wheels" structure. As with Level 5, students will perform four shows on the iO stages.

Level 7 – Graduate Level – Create Your Own Show features an instructor as coach who helps your "team" to create a new improv form/show, which is performed seven times on the iO stages.

UCB West

Much like the East Coast theater, UCB West is all about the game of the scene. The training program very closely mirrors the New York school (see above), with some additional electives that are more focused on the LA market.

The Second City

As with UCB and iO, The Second City in Hollywood is built upon the same philosophical framework as the Chicago theater, with a more heavily focused curriculum in film and television. As with the Chicago theater, there are classes in a variety of topics on the comedy continuum – more so than most other schools – but let's simply look at the improv curriculum, which features three levels and a Conservatory.

Improv 1 – Improvising Basics
Improv 2 – Improvising Characters
Improv 3 – Improvising Scenes

After these three levels, students are eligible to audition for the Conservatory, which trains students on how to put together a Second City-style revue.

Conservatory 1 – Advanced Ensemble Improvisation
Conservatory 2 – Characters
Conservatory 3 – Character Within Scene Work
Conservatory 4 – Styles, Genres, and Scene Type
Conservatory 5A – Political and Social Satire
Conservatory 5B – Creating an Original Second City-style Revue.

ACME Comedy

While not an exclusive improv theater, ACME Comedy does offer a wide array of courses in improvisation and sketch comedy, as well as courses in sitcom writing and stand-up. The two-course improv curriculum is done in conjunction with Carolyne Barry Creative Entertainment.

There is an Intro to Improv course for those with no improv experience, but most students who have done college-level improv will jump into Performance Improv Level 1 and 2. Both levels feature class performances, but Level 2 is by invitation only.

Other Improv Schools

Improv is hardly a Chicago, New York, Los Angeles art form. It exists pretty much everywhere. Here are some of the leading schools not in one of the aforementioned cities, but still very much worth considering if you happen to live in the other 99% of the country. As noted above, there are many, many more schools than we have listed, so poke around, ask about, and see shows at the improv theater(s) in your city.

The Brave New Workshop

One of the oldest improv theaters in the country, The Brave New Workshop Student Union in Minneapolis, MN offers training in improvisation and sketch comedy in a self-proclaimed "creative gymnasium." There is an Everyday Improv track for those with little background, and an audition-based Performance Track for those serious about studying comedy. Each level ends with a performance.

Performance Level 1 focuses on the skills necessary to build a strong scene and starts at a higher level than the typical "intro" class.
Performance Level 2 builds on scene work and skills used for heightening scenes.
Performance Level 3 introduces long form structures, such as LaRonde, Deconstruction, and The Movie.
Performance Level 4 centers on the Harold.

HUGE Theater

Another Minneapolis school, HUGE Theater has four levels that are designed to focus on scene work and long form improv. HUGE allows students to "transfer" credit from other schools, so students who study at BNW, for instance, don't have to start at Level 1.

101 (Here's Where to Start): This is your traditional intro to improv level with a focus on the basics.
201 (Characters): Focusing on creating and sustaining characters, this level also introduces basic scene work skills such as patterns, game, editing, etc.
301 (Scene work): This builds on the scenic skills of 201, and works on group scenes, split scenes, and traditional and non-traditional editing forms.

400 Levels: Students begin with a three-week Forms Essential class, then transition into three-week pods that each focus on a particular long form structure.

DSI Comedy Theater

Located in Carrboro, NC, DSI hosts the North Carolina Comedy Arts Festival and is one of the most well-respected improv theaters in the country. Their improv training curriculum features seven levels and focuses on building strong scenes.

The titles of the classes pretty much sum it up:

Improv 101: Fundamentals of Improv Comedy
Improv 201: Characters and Relationships
Improv 301: Game of the Scene and Patterns
Improv 401: Harold, Introduction to the Form
Improv 501: Harold, Advanced Techniques
Improv 601: Performance Forms – students explore a variety of non-Harold long form structures
Improv 701: Performance Classes – students must complete 601 and audition for 701. Students then work to create shows and performances.

The Improv Shop

A relatively new theater, The Improv Shop in St. Louis, MO is the city's only long form theater. Most of their instructors are Chicago-trained improvisers, so they bring a Chicago sensibility without the sense of "improv as a stepping stone to something bigger" that can be found in many Chicago improvisers and students (not that this is a bad thing as most contemporary comedy is heavily influenced by improvisation). There are five levels in the curriculum, with an optional Level 0 for folks with little to no experience.

Level 1 – Introduction to Long Form Improvisation presents the building blocks of improv.
Level 2 – Scene Work begins building the fundamentals for two-person and group scenes through listening and the game of the scene.
Level 3 – Harold introduces students to the classic form. Students perform a Harold during an evening performance at the end of the class.

Level 4 – Forms Survey builds on the Harold and introduces students to other long form structures.

Level 5 – Performance features students developing their own structure/show, which will be performed four times.

The New Movement

With theaters in New Orleans, LA and Austin, TX, The New Movement offers classes in improvisation and sketch comedy. They also offer Training Camps several times throughout the year that are two-week intensives featuring nightly performances aimed at professional and collegiate improvisers. The traditional five-level curriculum is focused on character, the game of the scene, patterns, and scenic devices, with special emphasis placed on the beginning of scenes and using that material throughout the scene. Read more in TNM's book *Improv Wins!*.

ImprovBoston

Another theater with a long tradition, ImprovBoston focuses its energy on the many ways comedy is produced. Students have the opportunity to attend classes in improv, sketch comedy, and stand-up, as well as attending some of ImprovBoston's nationally acclaimed master classes.

The Improv curriculum features six levels.

Improv 101 explores the fundamentals of scene work, introducing techniques that develop trust, support, and agreement.

Improv 201 digs into the two-person scene, identifying the game of the scene and developing patterns, themes, and story.

Improv 301 provides an introduction to Harold, the classic long form format, training students to focus and actively support the ensemble.

Improv 401 focuses on the development of group mind, as well as the creation of thematically cohesive shows.

Improv 501 applies Harold skills to the execution of many other popular long form structures.

Improv 601 draws upon everything students master in a year of improv classes to create an original long form show.

For those who are musically inclined, ImprovBoston also provides 101–301 classes for musical improvisation. Comedy Drop-Ins, held almost every Saturday of the year, are a great way to get a well-rounded improv experience, allowing students to take multiple classes in different comedic fields.

PHIT (Philly Improv Theatre)

Offering its first class in 2005, PHIT, home of Philly's long form improv scene, has continuously offered top-rate small classes. PHIT makes it a point that improv isn't just for actors – the skills learned in an improv class can be translated to all aspects of your life.

The improv curriculum features four levels.

Improv 101 teaches the basic improv concept of "Yes, And" and shows how a scene can be created through agreement as well as creating characters, establishing relationships, exploring scenes with objects, and environment work.

Improv 102 reinforces scene work exercises that aim to strengthen and work the core improv concepts while building on relationships, location, and emotional point of view.

Improv 201 teaches students how to recognize and build on patterns to advance their scenes. Students will also begin to learn elements of structure for performance and create fully improvised scenes with more than two performers.

Improv 202 aims to reinforce the concepts taught in the previous week's Improv 201 class. Each practice group will include warm-ups and scene work exercises that will aid students with their improvisational exploration.

Improv 301 helps improvisers to continue building on skills acquired in prior levels through use of new acting techniques and additional improv formats, with a heavy focus on individual attention from their instructor.

Improv 302 serves as a practice session with a scene work focus for advanced improvisers. These sessions ensure you end up with a much more productive experience that places you with fellow improvisers of equivalent level.

Improv 401 is an introduction to "The Harold," allowing students to build on their understandings of patterns and also learn to perform in scenes with large groups.

Improv electives, one-day improv workshops, and master classes are also offered.

205

ComedySportz

ComedySportz is a national short form improv chain with theaters in over 20 cities. Each individual theater has a slightly different array of classes, but all focus on the high-energy, fast and furious ComedySportz style. If you are interested in short form improv, you'll probably want to start taking classes at ComedySportz. Just for reference, we've included the classes at the Philadelphia branch (which is the one closest to us here at Albright College).

> ComedySportz 00: Open House – Like several other theaters on the list, ComedySportz offers a free introductory course designed for folks with little experience.
>
> Improv 101: Introduction to Improv – The basic intro-level course that focuses on developing basic improv skills.
>
> Improv 201: Introduction to Scenework – Using short form games, this class focuses on developing scenes.
>
> Improv 203: Introduction to Long Form Improv – focusing on creating longer scenes and forms by building relationships, this class offers an intro to long form techniques.
>
> Improv 301: Advanced Improv – this class builds on 201, and teaches a number of ComedySportz games. This class usually has an informal performance at the end.
>
> Improv 302: Intro to Musical Improv – this class focuses on developing musical skills both for short form singing games, and for use in long form scenes.
>
> Improv 401: Expert Improv – this level is all about refining your skills and learning what it takes to make a successful Comedy Sportz show.

The Loose Moose Theatre Company

Founded by Keith Johnstone in Calgary, Canada, and based on his improvisational teachings, The Loose Moose Theatre Company is internationally recognized and the leading Theatresports institution in the world. They provide introductory classes, but are best known for the International Improvisation School that is held every summer. The school is aimed at both performers and teachers, and brings together improvisers from around the world. While the program goes over fundamentals, it is aimed at more advanced students, and explores improvisation in many ways, including contact improvisation and improvised scenography. The program also pulls on the strengths and expertise of the participants, offering them opportunities to exchange ideas and exercises with one another.

BATS (Bay Area Theatresports)

Tracing its origins back to Keith Johnstone, BATS students are taught improvisation in the form of games, using competition as dramatic effect in regard to the performance aspect.

The improv curriculum features three foundation classes (each consisting of a six-week series).

> Foundation 1 introduces students to the basics of improv through games and exercises in a safe, friendly atmosphere. Concepts include spontaneity, listening, storytelling, status, and making one's partner look good.
> Foundation 2 continues the exploration of improvisation while focusing even more on scene work.
> Foundation 3 continues the study of scene work, ensemble, character, acting, and other advanced improv.

At the end of Foundation 3, the coach will make a recommendation for each student about what next step is best for them – repeating Foundation 3 or moving to Studio Scenework, a more performance-oriented scene study class.

BATS also provides Improv Off-Stage which includes classes for shy people, singles, caregivers, teachers, or facilitators.

SAKS Comedy Lab

Located in Orlando, FL, SAKS Comedy Lab is one of the oldest improv comedy theaters in the country, most notable for launching Wayne Brady's career. SAKS University offers a four-level curriculum in improvisation.

> Level 1 is the basic introductory course that teaches the skills and language of improvisation.
> Level 2 builds on the lessons of Level 1 and begins exploring more advanced techniques and learning more games.
> Level 3 focuses on creating strong relationship-based scenes with strong emotional dynamics.

207

Level 4 is a performance track class that is designed to prepare students for the graduation show. Students focus on performance games and skills needed to carry out a successful show.

SAK Advanced Conservatory is a ten-week program that introduces long form and continues building scenic skills.

The Comedy Store Players Improvisation Academy

One of London's leading improv schools, The Improvisation Academy provides training that is designed to carry you beyond the stage. Using an Applied Improvisation approach, the course work is divided into Improvisation for Life and Improvisation at Work, focusing on personal and professional development. There are four levels for each:

Improvisation for Life features courses in Confidence Building, Communication Skills, Creativity, and Performing.
Improvisation at Work features courses in Resilience, Presentation Skills, Teamwork and Leadership, and Problem Solving.

208

Conclusion

If you are still reading this handbook, chances are that you now know a lot more about improv than you did on page 1. Congratulations! Call your mother. She still misses you. Your father is more than likely still at Buffalo Wild Wings… drowning his disillusionment with you in wings. If you don't take anything else from this book, remember this:

Have fun.

Take risks.

And be nice to one another.

209

Your Improv Library

Adams, Kenn. *How to Improvise a Full-Length Play: The Art of Spontaneous Theater*. New York: Allworth Press, 2007.

Arkin, Alan. *An Improvised Life: A Memoir*. Philadelphia: Da Capo Press, 2011.

Boal, Augusto. *Theatre of the Oppressed*. New York: Theatre Communications Group, 1985.

Boal, Augusto. *Games for Actors and Non-Actors, 2nd Edition*. London: Routledge, 2002.

Bogart, Anne, and Tina Landau. *The Viewpoints Book: A Practical Guide to Viewpoints and Composition*. New York: Theatre Communications Group, 2004.

Book, Stephen. *Book on Acting: Improvisation Technique for the Professional Actor in Film, Theater, and Television*. Los Angeles: Silman-James Press, 2002.

Boyd, Neva Leona. *Play and Game Theory in Group Work: A Collection of Papers*. Chicago: University of Illinois at Chicago Circle, 1971.

Carrane, Jimmy. *Improv Therapy: How to Get Out of Your Own Way to Become a Better Improviser*. Amazon Digital Services, 2014.

Carrane, Jimmy and Liz Allen. *Improvising Better: A Guide for the Working Improviser*. Portsmouth, NH: Heinemann, 2006.

Charles, David Alfred. *The Novelty of Improvisation: Towards a Genre of Embodied Spontaneity*. PhD dissertation, 2003, available at: http://etd.lsu.edu/docs/available/etd-0701103-135033/unrestricted/Charles_dis.pdf

Chin, Jason. *Long Form Improvisation and the Art of Zen: A Manual for Advanced Performers*. Bloomington, IN: New York: iUniverse, Inc., 2009.

Coleman, Janet. *The Compass: The Improvisational Theatre that Revolutionized American Comedy*. Chicago: University of Chicago Press, 1990.

Cook, William. *The Comedy Store: The Club That Changed British Comedy*. New York: Little, Brown & Co., 2011.

Davis, Andrew. *Baggy Pants Comedy: Burlesque and the Oral Tradition*. New York: Palgrave Macmillan, 2011.

Diggles, Dan. *Improv for Actors*. New York: Allworth Press, 2004.

Fey, Tina. *Bossypants*. New York: Reagan Arthur Books, 2011.

Fisher, James. *The Theatre of Yesterday and Tomorrow: Commedia Dell'arte on the Modern Stage*. Lewiston, NY: E Mellen Press, 1992.

Foreman, Kathleen, and Clem Martini. *Something Like a Drug: An Unauthorized Oral History of Theatresports*. Alberta, Canada: Red Deer College Press, 1995.

Frost, Anthony, and Ralph Yarrow. *Improvisation in Drama, 2nd edition*. New York: Palgrave MacMillan, 2007.

Gilbert, Douglas. *American Vaudeville: Its Life and Times*. New York: Dover Pubs, 1963.

Goldberg, Andy. *Improv Comedy*. New York: Samuel French, 1991.

Goodman, Katie. *Improvisation for the Spirit: Live a More Creative, Spontaneous, and Courageous Life Using the Tools of Improvisation*. Naperville, IL: Sourcebooks, Inc., 2008.

Griggs, Jeff. *Guru: My Days with Del Close*. Chicago: Ivan R. Dee, 2005.

Gwinn, Peter and Charna Halpern. *Group Improvisation: The Manual of Ensemble Improv Games*. Colorado Springs, CO: Meriwether Publishing, 2003.

Halpern, Charna. *Art by Committee: A Guide to Advanced Improvisation*. Colorado Springs, CO: Meriwether Publishing, 2006.

211

Halpern, Charna, Del Close, and Kim "Howard" Johnson. *Truth in Comedy: The Manual of Improvisation*. Colorado Springs, CO: Meriwether Publishing, 1994.

Hazenfield, Carol. *Acting on Impulse: The Art of Making Improv Theater*. Berkeley, CA: Coventry Creek Press, 2002.

Hicks, Margaret. *Chicago Comedy: A Fairly Serious History*. Charleston, SC: The History Press, 2011.

Horn, Delton T. *Comedy Improvisation: Exercises & Techniques for Young Actors*. Colorado Springs, CO: Meriwether Publishing, 1992.

Izzo, Gary. *The Art of Play: The New Genre of Interactive Theatre*. Portsmouth, NH: Heinemann, 1997.

Jagodowski, T.J., David Pasquesi, and Pam Victor. *Improvisation at the Speed of Life: The TJ and Dave Book*. New York: Solo Roma, Inc., 2015.

Johnson, David Read, and Renee Emunah (eds). *Current Approaches in Drama Therapy*. Springfield, IL: Charles C Thomas Publisher, 2009.

Johnson, Kim "Howard." *The Funniest One in the Room: The Lives and Legends of Del Close*. Chicago: Chicago Review Press, 2008.

Johnstone, Keith. *Impro for Storytellers*. New York: Faber and Faber, 1998.

Johnstone, Keith. *Impro: Improvisation and the Theatre*. New York: Routledge, 1989.

Kaplan, Steve. *The Hidden Tools of Comedy: The Serious Business of Being Funny*. Studio City, CA: Michael Wiese Productions, 2013.

Kozlowski, Rob. *The Art of Chicago Improv: Shortcuts to Long-Form Improvisation*. Portsmouth, NH: Heinemann, 2002.

Lecoq, Jacques. *The Moving Body: Teaching Creative Theatre*. New York: Routledge, 2001.

Leep, Jeanne. *Theatrical Improvisation: Short Form, Long Form, and Sketch-Based Improv*. New York: Palgrave Macmillan, 2008.

Leonard, Kelly, and Tom Yorton. *Yes, And: How Improvisation Reverses "No, But" Thinking and Improves Creativity and Collaboration—Lessons from The Second City*. New York: HarperBusiness, 2015.

Libera, Anne. *The Second City Almanac of Improvisation*. Evanston, IL: Northwestern University Press, 2004.

Lynn, Bill. *Improvisation for Actors and Writers: A Guidebook for Improv Lessons in Comedy*. Colorado Springs, CO: Meriwether Publishing, 2004.

Madson, Patricia Ryan. *Improv Wisdom: Don't Prepare, Just Show Up*. New York: Bell Tower, 2005.

McCrohan, Donna. *The Second City: A Backstage History of Comedy's Hottest Troupe*. New York: Perigee, 1987.

McKnight, Katherine S., and Mary Scruggs. *The Second City Guide to Improv in the Classroom: Using Improvisation to Teach Skills and Boost Learning*. San Francisco: Jossey-Bass, 2008.

Moreno, Jonathan. *Impromptu Man: J.L. Moreno and the Origins of Psychodrama, Encounter Culture, and the Social Network*. New York: Bellevue Literary Press, 2014.

Napier, Mick. *Improvise: Scene From the Inside Out*. Portsmouth, NH: Heinemann, 2004.

Nevraumont, Edward, Nicholas Hanson, and Kurt Smeaton. *The Ultimate Improv Book: A Complete Guide to Comedy Improvisation*. Colorado Springs, CO: Meriwether Publishing, 2002.

Norman, Rob. *Improvising Now*. CreateSpace Independent Publishing Platform, 2014.

Patikin, Sheldon. *The Second City: Backstage at the World's Greatest Comedy Theatre*. Naperville, IL: Sourcebooks, Inc., 2000.

Peters, Gary. *The Philosophy of Improvisation*. Chicago: University of Chicago Press, 2009.

Poehler, Amy. *Yes Please*. New York: Dey Street Books, 2014.

Pollack, Michael. *Musical Direction for Improv and Sketch Comedy*. Hollywood, CA: Masteryear Publishing, 2005.

Pollack, Michael and Jason Alexander. *Musical Improv Comedy: Creating Songs in the Moment*. Gardena, CA: SCB Distributors, 2004.

Raftery, Brian. *High-Status Characters: How The Upright Citizens Brigade Stormed a City, Started a Scene, and Changed Comedy Forever*. New York: Megawatt Press, 2013.

Robbins, Jeff. *Second City Television: A History and Episode Guide*. Jefferson, NC: McFarland Publishing, 2007.

Robbins Dudeck, Theresa. *Keith Johnstone: A Critical Biography*. London: Bloomsbury Methuen Drama, 2013.

Sacks, Mike. *Poking a Dead Frog: Conversations with Today's Top Comedy Writers*. New York: Penguin Books, 2014.

Sahlins, Bernard. *Days and Nights at the Second City: A Memoir, with Notes on Staging Review Theatre*. Chicago: Ivan R. Dee, 2001.

Salinsky, Tom and Deborah Frances-White. *The Improv Handbook: The Ultimate Guide to Improvising in Comedy, Theatre, and Beyond*. New York: Continuum International Publishing Group, 2008.

Schindler, Carol and Tom Soter. *A Doctor and a Plumber in a Rowboat: The Essential Guide to Improvisation*. CreateSpace Independent Publishing Platform, 2014.

Scruggs, Mary and Michael Gellman. *Process: An Improviser's Journey*. Evanston, IL: Northwestern University Press, 2008.

Seham, Amy. *Whose Improv is it Anyway? Beyond Second City*. Jackson, MS: University Press of Mississippi, 2001.

Smith, Tom. *The Other Blocking: Teaching and Performing Improvisation*. Dubuque, IA: Kendall/Hunt Publishing Company, 2009.

Spolin, Viola. *Improvisation for the Theatre, 3rd edition*. Evanston, IL: Northwestern University Press, 1999.

Spolin, Viola. *Theater Games for Rehearsal: A Director's Handbook*. Evanston, IL: Northwestern University Press, 2011.

213

Spolin, Viola. *Theater Games for the Classroom: A Teacher's Handbook*. Evanston, IL: Northwestern University Press, 1986.

Spolin, Viola. *Theater Games for the Lone Actor*. Evanston, IL: Northwestern University Press, 2001.

Sweeney, John, and The Brave New Workshop. *Innovation at the Speed of Laughter: 8 Secrets to World Class Idea Generation*. Andover, MN: Expert Publishing, Inc., 2004.

Sweet, Jeffrey. *Something Wonderful Right Away: An Oral History of The Second City and The Compass Players*. New York: Avon Books, 1978.

Tharp, Twyla. *The Creative Habit: Learn It and Use It for Life*. New York: Simon & Schuster, 2006.

Thomas, Dave. *SCTV: Behind the Scenes*. Toronto, Canada: McClelland & Stewart, 1997.

Thomas, Mike. *The Second City Unscripted: Revolution and Revelation at the World-Famous Comedy Theater*. New York: Villard Books, 2009.

Vorhaus, John. *The Comic Toolbox: How to be Funny Even if You're Not*. Los Angeles: Silman-James Press, 1994.

Walsh, Matt, Ian Roberts, and Matt Besser. *Upright Citizens Brigade Comedy Improvisation Manual*. New York: Comedy Council of Nicea, 2013.

Weitz, Eric. *The Cambridge Introduction to Comedy*. Cambridge: Cambridge University Press, 2009.

Wirth, Jeff. *Interactive Acting: Acting, Improvisation, and Interacting for Audience Participatory Theatre*. Fall Creek, OR: Fall Creek Press, 1994.

Zaunbrecher, Nicolas J. "The Elements of Improvisation: Structural Tools for Spontaneous Theatre." *Theatre Topics*. 21, no. 1 (March 2011): 49–59.

214

Index

219

220